GREENSPAN'S
TAMING
OF THE
WAVE

To Maïa, Guillaume et Aude

'If you were forced to try to narrow down the credit for the golden age that we find ourselves living in . . . I think your name would have to be at the top of the list,' said Senate Banking Chairman Phil Gramm, setting the session's tone.

Wall Street Journal, 27 January 2000

(Phil Gramm's welcome address to the US Senate Banking Committee on Greenspan's nomination to a fourth term as Chairman of the US Federal Reserve, 26 January 2000)

GREENSPAN'S TAMING OF THE WAVE

NEW STORMS CHALLENGING THE NEW ECONOMY

FRANÇOIS-XAVIER CHEVALLIER

KOGAN
PAGE

First published in paperback 2002

Kogan Page Ltd
120 Pentonville Road
London N1 9JN
www.kogan-page.co.uk

© English language edition Kogan Page 2000

Original French language edition (Le bonheur économique)
© Editions Albin Michel S.A. Paris 1998

British Library Cataloguing in Publication Data

A CIP record for this book is available from the British Library

ISBN 0 7494 3749 9

Designed and typeset by JS Typesetting, Wellingborough, Northamptonshire
Printed and bound in Great Britain by Creative Print and Design, Ebbw Vale, Wales

Contents

Acknowledgements   viii

Foreword by Edward S Hyman   x

Preface to the revised English edition   xi

Prologue: Thank You, Asia!   xvii
Long waves and short-term cycles: what is it all about?   xxii

Part One: The Marvellous Clock   1

1   The Theory of the Long Cycle   7
    The price cycle   7
    The production cycle   11
    The long wave and the life cycle   17

2   Modelling the Relationships Between Production,
    Prices and Debt: A Long Wave Approach   23
    The lag between prices and production   23
    The peak of inflation halfway through the production
    plateau   24
    Identification of the feel-good era or speculative prosperity 26
    Introduction of the debt cycle: Irving Fisher's model   29

3   The Test of History and the Pressure of the Current
    State of Affairs   33
    The chronology of the three preceding cycles   34
    A cross-sectional or thematic approach to the long waves   39
    Is there such thing as a fourth Kondratieff cycle: 1937 to
    1997?   43
    Why the 1973 to 1997 period qualifies as the down wave of
    the latest cycle   45

**Part Two: The Magnificent Parallels Between the
Third and Fourth Cycles and Why Our Depression is
Waning**   47

4   **A Parallel Between the 1910s And The 1970s:
Stagflation Time**   51

The abandonment of monetary discipline and the
explosion of inflation   53

The rise of antagonisms and the race for real assets   54

5   **Parallel between the 1920s and the 1980s: Variations
on the Theme of the Feel-Good Era Leading to a
Financial Bubble**   59

Parallel with the 1920s: initiation   60

Anecdotal similarities   61

Disinflation and the tide of debt   64

Rise and fall of the financial sphere   67

6   **The Crash of 1990 or Burst of the Japanese Bubble
as a Resounding Echo of the Crash of 1929**   75

Marvellous precision of Kondratieff's clock: critical zone,
margin of error and catalyst   76

Margin of error and critical zone   77

What would be the catalyst for the Japanese crash?   79

Timing, the king's prerogative: but which king?   80

7   **Parallel Between the 1930s and the 1990s, or the
Negative Aspect of this Ongoing 'Creative
Destruction'**   87

The Japanese depression: illustration and textbook case of
Fisher's model   88

An escalation in the penalties incurred: Japan, Europe,
United States   93

Influence of the stabilizers: is there such a thing as a 'soft
depression'?   97

A sequence of magnificent parallels   104

**Part Three: Creative Destruction or the Positive
Side of Depression**   **107**

**8   The Depression Myths and Realities: Fruitfulness
of the Depression**   **109**
Depression as a myth   110
A regulatory function   112
Fruitfulness of the depression   114
Every cloud has a silver lining (or Seeds of the rebound
in creative destruction)   117

9   De-leveraging and the Ideal of Popular Capitalism   **121**
Necessary de-leveraging   122
Precursory role of corporations   122
Private individuals, in turn . . .   123
Governments themselves on the way to budgetary
orthodoxy   125
The ideal of popular capitalism   128

10   Signs that the Downwave is Over   **135**
Concrete economic signs   136
A technological revolution comparable in scope with
the invention of the printing press   141
Geopolitical revolution: the extension of development to
a new set of countries is not called into question by the
Asian crisis   143

**Conclusion: Breaking the Waves with Alan Greenspan:
Tomorrow, the Next Up Wave**   **147**

Epilogue: Alan Greenspan's brave new world   **153**

**Appendix I: Relationship between the business cycle
and interest rates**   **157**

Appendix II: Interview, *Paris Match*, 2 August 1990   **159**

Bibliography   **161**

Index   **167**

Acknowledgements

It took long years of research for this book's leading ideas to mature, rooted as they are in the daily observation of economic realities, as much as in the theoretical apparatus which supports them. They have crystallized slowly, whilst benefiting from discussions with leading experts. A few of them were especially instrumental in my investigations and need be singled out here with great emphasis. Ed Hyman, one of Wall Street's favourite economists, deserves a special tribute in this regard, for he repeatedly fed my appetite for factual evidence concerning long waves. Although he seldom openly mentions long cycles, I feel he constantly keeps thinking of them in the back of his mind. I have known him for more than twenty years now, and have immensely benefited from his deep and unique insight in the way the US and world economies work. As his personal qualities match his outstanding intellectual foresight, over the years I dare say he has become a friend. Thus my warmest personal regards and thanks first extend to him and his wonderful family, his wife Caroline, and kids Prue, Mac and Curtis. Needless to say, I wish him and his associates at ISI, notably Nancy Lazar, a prolonged extension of his own success . . . at least throughout the next Kondratieff wave.

I also feel indebted to Michel Lutfalla, one of the most famous French specialists in long wave theory and AXA group Chief Economist, and who, in the late seventies, opened up for me the editorial columns of *La Revue d'économie politique*. Ten years ago, he helped me elaborate an earlier and unpublished version of this book entitled *Are we on the verge of a new crash? Chronicle of an anticipated crisis 1990–2000*. In hindsight, that one was not only premonitory but unexpectedly accurate in its predictions.

For earlier drafts of this book, I benefited a lot from the patient comments of Gérard Bekerman, a Finance professor at Paris-Assas, whose intellectual rigour and constructive bias have been of great help.

Further out in time, I want to express my deep gratitude to my former high-school masters from the Lycée Chateaubriand in Rennes, Brittany, especially Messrs Pestel, Gouallou, Massiot, Montpert, Lagoutte, Richard and Crenn. Although they were civil servants, no other private professor could have been more dedicated to their task. I feel also *over-indebted* to some of my University of Chicago professors, for they helped me assert in my mind an irresistible taste for economics and finance, which Alain Cotta had already aroused at HEC years before. My thoughts are especially dedicated to a few great names of the Chicago School. In retrospect, I feel incredibly lucky to have been taught directly, at the source, both monetarism by Milton Friedman and supply-side economics by Arthur Laffer, not to mention the theory of finance by Merton Miller, Eugene Fama and the late Fisher Black.

How could I have realized back then in 1971–73, that these five academic stars were about to reshape the world of economics and finance for the rest of the century, and probably far beyond? In that sense, Art Laffer probably deserves a special mention here, for I sincerely believe that no other economist ever had a greater influence on his time, from the Reagan and Thatcher years to start with, and the aftermath of the fall of the Berlin Wall to beyond, with its built-in 'economic consequences of the peace', as Ed Yardeni put it. My best personal and respectful regards extend to him and his family, as I have been lucky enough to remain closely in touch with him, not only benefiting from his great insight into world affairs, but also continuing to exchange views with him on a personal basis.

Let me also express my gratitude to my colleagues and friends at BNP Asset Management, especially Gilles de Vaugrigneuse, Arnaud Maspétiol, Philippe d'Arvisenet, Guy Longueville and Claude Maréchal, for they make my professional life rich and stimulating, and have viewed this project positively. I am also grateful to Frederique Bonnell and Wanda Rutyna, who helped design the Excel versions of some of the original charts.

Lastly, the French original version of this book owes a lot to Bernard Maris, whose enlightened advice, intellectual rigour and human qualities have helped me greatly in shaping it up in its present form.

According to the ritual formula, all errors remain mine, and only I remain accountable for its central message.

Foreword

François Chevallier has produced in this work an extremely useful framework for better understanding developments of the past decade, for analysing the current picture and forecasting future economic and market trends. In my view, it is imperative to place today's global economy and markets in a longer-term perspective, which is what this work does so well.

I have worked with François for 20 years and have found him to be one of the most original thinkers in the investment business. Perhaps better than anyone, he combines a deep understanding of current economic and market developments with brilliant insights into long cycles. Over the years, his thinking has been enlightened and I have learned much from it. At the same time, François and his family have become treasured friends.

Edward S. Hyman
Chairman, ISI Group, Inc.

Preface to the Revised English Edition

New Storms Challenging the New Economy

This book's thesis is that Alan Greenspan's incredible track record as Chairman of the Federal Reserve over the last 14 years is at least partially attributable to his thorough knowledge and understanding of both long wave cycles and Irving Fisher's debt deflation approach of depressions. Russian economist Kondratieff's long wave theory (1925) states that the world economy basically follows a cyclical pattern with 30-year up waves followed by down waves of about equal length. Since the Industrial Revolution took off in Britain in the early 1780s in the aftermath of the US Independence War, four such cycles have already unfolded, with an average length of 56 years. As for Irving Fisher's contribution, we have narrowed it down to his claim that inflation and over-indebtedness are 'the two evils' (and the only two) impeding growth. Although Kondratieff initially documented his theory on the price cycle only, implicitly assuming that prices and quantities (production) moved synchronously in concert, by combining the two theories we were able to demonstrate that a full Kondratieff wave in fact has three components, or three sub-cycles, with a seven to ten year lag between them: production, inflation and indebtedness.

The beauty of this new theory is that it breaks down a full 56-year cycle into five seasons depending on where we stand in terms of the relative position of the three variables. The five seasons are the following: Autumn (eg the 1973–80 stagflation), Indian Summer (the financial bubble of the 1980s) ending in a stockmarket crash (Tokyo 1990), Winter (the 1991–95 creative destruction phase), Spring (the 1995–2001 beginnings of the New Economy), and lastly Summer, or mature prosperity (latest known: 1960–70s and forthcoming: 2002–2020?).

Winter is the toughest and most critical of all, as it is both the tail end of an ongoing Kondratieff down wave and the transition phase towards (or prelude to) the next up wave. Occurring in the aftermath of a market crash, this 'creative destruction' phase is triggered by debt deflation forces which, if left unchecked, tend to push the banking system into bankruptcy through an unusual weight of delinquency loans, and may eventually lead to a real economy depression (eg the 1930s in the US or the 1990s in Japan). Irving Fisher had stated in the 1930s that depressions were avoidable, and had given hints on how to achieve that goal.

Over the entire span of his tenure at the helm of the Federal Reserve, a few storms have repeatedly challenged Alan Greenspan's credibility. However, each and every single time such a challenge occurred, he success-fully addressed it, thus demonstrating his unusual grip over the three long wave *seasons* he has presided over to date. We believe this amazing understanding of economic history and of long waves in particular must have been crucial, amongst other things, to his success. How did we guess this was the case?

The first hint is the way he quickly tackled the 1987 crash in the latest known *Indian Summer* (of the 1980s), at a time when most people feared the 1929 spectre was looming again. Then we knew he was ready to take advantage of the lessons of the past and not to let history completely repeat itself in the United States. Second, in the *Winter* season of the early 1990s, in sharp contrast to what his Japanese counterpart did at the same time, he quickly solved the US Savings and Loans problem, thereby validating Irving Fisher's hypothesis that depressions are avoidable. This is exactly when we felt Alan Greenspan must have read Irving Fisher's 1935 'Theory of Debt Deflation Led Crashes and Depressions'. Not only was depression avoided in the 1990s in the US, but Greenspan strongly contributed to turn those times into kick-starting the New Economy to the great benefit of the United States, whilst carefully steering his country clear of those two antagonistic pitfalls of deflation and inflation. Hence this third hint, again in the *Winter* season, when he abruptly put an end to the 1994 overheating threat to the US economy, whilst suddenly raising short rates from 3 per cent to 6 per cent within a few months at the risk of triggering a bond market crash that year. 'Make no mistake,' he could have argued, 'I am no inflation dove'. Back then, he must have felt the New Economy was brewing, and he would not let that great opportunity be missed. . .

When *Spring* (the New Economy) at long last materialized in the mid-1990s, he did not allow the Asian crisis, nor the LTCM story one year later, to choke it off. This was our fourth hint.

The last and most explicit one, however, was the way he started, back in 1997–98, to elaborate at length in his testimonies about the impact of the IT revolution on the US business cycle. This argument is crucial because Kondratieff himself had always stressed that technical innovation was the most important ingredient for the beginning of a new up wave. Anyway, starting in 1998, most of Greenspan's official speeches would systematically refer to 'the productivity gains and their impact on the unusual length of this expansion', and to 'parallels with other technical innovations from the past: the railways, electricity. . .' He even repeatedly alluded to the long-wave driven periodicity of such technological path-breaking discoveries 'every 50 to 100 years'. Could he have been more explicit? At some stage, in an October 1999 speech delivered in Boca Raton, Alan Greenspan went as far as borrowing from Lou Gerstner, then Chairman of IBM, that 'we were only five years into a thirty-year cycle of technological change'. Judging from this reference alone, it seems that the Fed Chief's impressive track record must have owed a lot to his inner conviction that, starting in the early 1990s, the down wave that had plagued the industrial world since the 1973 Oil Shock was coming to an end. More explicitly, he probably felt the ominous balance-sheet and over-leverage problems that fell upon the industrialized world in those days were doing nothing but pave the way for the next Kondratieff up wave, provided the right decisions were made. And this vision, which no other political authority nor central banker shared at the time, must have given him the self-confidence he needed to move ahead in a creative way, often against all odds, sometimes with and sometimes against the gods. All in all, and paraphrasing Phill Gramm's welcome address to the Fed Chairman for his nomination for a fourth term at the Fed on 26 January 2000, we could say: 'If anybody deserved to be credited for the golden age the industrialized world found itself living in at the turn of the millennium, Alan Greenspan's name would have to be at the top of the list'.

This official recognition by the US Congress that Alan Greenspan could be identified with a golden age also sounded like a confirmation to us that we were in the right direction. But we had to be careful using the phrase 'golden age'. To us it simply meant a period of accelerating growth with inflation held in check. There is no way it meant the advent of 'a brave new world' of perfect harmony. Hence our epilogue, mostly borrowed from *The Tempest*, where Prospero's lucidity is in sharp contrast with his daughter Miranda's dreams. What we meant there was the new up wave would not be immune from business cycle recessions. In short, our admiration for Greenspan's track record would fall short of his deification. And we were ready to consider new storms on the horizon to challenge the new economy.

Hence to our surprise, even before the September 11 events hit an already ailing US economy, a strong minority of observers and economists openly questioned whether our modern Prospero had lost his magic touch. This was very much like asking what was left of the New Economy. To shape up our interpretation of the facts, we must carefully distinguish the pre-September 11 situation from the post-September 11 outcome.

Previously, on two occasions in 1997 and 1998 as recalled above, the New Economy had been threatened by exogenous factors: the Asian crisis on the one hand, the Russian financial collapse and the LTCM story on the other. Before the September events, we claimed that this time around, the New Economy had met its first endogenous threat, or in traditional terms, its first business cycle adjustment due to an over-investment and inventory excess in the IT sector. Because the rest of the economy was doing fine, we estimated that US GDP growth could still amount to 1.5 per cent in 2001 before recovering to a stronger 3.2 per cent pace in 2002. Nothing dramatic, no recession, just a soft landing. . .

The September drama has drastically altered this course of events from an economic and stockmarket standpoint. In the short term, because the Demand schedule has been pulled downwards, an outright, albeit mild, recession now seems unavoidable in the United States. However, this short-term 'air-pocket' will pave the way for a much steeper 'V-shaped' recovery than would otherwise have been the case, due to the formidable stimulus package the Bush administration has been working on – a Marshall Plan of some sort – and, again, to the Fed's swift response to the new situation. In economic terms, the recovery has been postponed by six months, from the turn of the year to the second quarter of 2002.

The stock market has already started to discount the forthcoming recovery, but the unusual and persistent threats lingering around the Western economies will probably demand a higher risk premium than would otherwise be the case, at least for the foreseeable future. So there is but little hope the equity risk premium could go back to its historical ten-year average. However, this still leaves room for further upside potential in the months ahead, despite the fact that the September 11 events have but little chance to remain a one-shot phenomenon.

Interestingly enough though, the Twin Towers drama also has a political connotation that can usefully be put in perspective within the golden age context. As expressed above, a golden age usually happens in the aftermath of a lengthy down wave in economic activity, through which accumulated frustrations from the poorer masses suddenly get exacerbated by this new prosperity. Hence, and paradoxically, golden ages are a propitious terrain for social unrest, or even revolution. Witness Bastille Day at the dawn of the Industrial Revolution, or the 1848 'Spring of the peoples' on the eve of the prosperous Victorian Era. Closer to us, the first Russian revolution of 1905 took place in the early stage of 'La Belle Époque', another spate of buoyant years, before World War I choked it off. Lastly, it is perhaps no mere coincidence that most African and Asian national liberation movements from former colonial powers took off in the mid-1950s during the 1945–73 up wave. Today, there is no doubt that the West-South wealth gap has widened over the last few years, as the benefits of globalization and Westernisation have not kept pace with the demographic trends of most Third World countries. 'Capitalizing' so to speak on this gap should be an easy task for ambitious demagogues eager to set up new political 'franchises' under whatever banner that appeals to these disenchanted masses. The good news about this historic parallel is that it is part of the long wave picture, and, to date, it never stopped up waves from unfolding. Paradoxically, there seems to be no golden age without blips of social unrest and revolutionary attempts. . .

All in all, from a historical perspective, and within a long wave framework, the September 11 drama can be seen as a remote echo of similar demonstrations of social unrest at this juncture of the long wave. Even if it is not reassuring in the short term, it is absolutely crucial to understand the roots of the phenomenon in order to address it properly. And the proper response is how do we boost growth and extend prosperity to the greatest number of people? How fast can we enlarge the club of developed countries to hold these revolutionary pulses in check? And, of course, from the terrorists' standpoint the reverse is true: the worse off the global economy the larger the clientele of frustrated people having nothing to lose. This accounts for the symmetry in economic strategies of both camps: the US camp is pro growth, pro business confidence, pro consumer confidence. The other side has the reverse strategy of spreading fear and anxiety, inhibiting consumption and investment, jeopardizing market confidence and abrogating wealth. Their strategy is to transform a West-South gap into a West-South confrontation, whereas the West's strategy is to try and fill the gap as soon as possible through pro growth, free market and free trade policies, among others. Since the September 11 shock, the Western coalition seems to have attracted more and more members, including Russia and China, not to mention a huge majority of Muslim States. This, in itself, is formidable good news and should, over time, dispel the clouds and storms threatening the New Economy.

François-Xavier Chevallier   November, 2001

Prologue
Thank You, Asia!

'Whether 'tis nobler in the mind to suffer the slings and arrows of outrageous fortune, or to take arms against a sea of troubles and by opposing end them . . .' (Hamlet, Act III, 3)

This book is a message of hope, for it foretells an extremely good piece of news: the very near, if not imminent, end of the long down wave initiated in 1973 by the oil crisis, and the forthcoming advent of a 30-year prosperity up-leg of the type previously experienced both during the 'belle époque' of 1883 to 1913 and the post-war 'miracle years' of 1945 to 1973. That is why this book is dedicated primarily to all those who have lost hope of finding a job and the status in society which goes with it. It is dedicated to all young people, especially in Europe and Japan, not to mention billions elsewhere, notably in Asia, who are anxious about their future, and who do not yet know how lucky they are to be nearing their working life at such a favourable turning point in the long cycle.

In the United States and Britain it is hard to admit that the industrial-ized world at large remains in a down wave given the 'golden age' benefits they themselves have enjoyed over the last few years. One tends to forget the 'headwinds' that Alan Greenspan referred to in the early 1990s when he so smartly addressed the savings and loans (S&L) crisis. But their recent and hard-won prosperity does not mean that they have been totally immune from the down wave; ask George Bush, US president and 1991 Desert Storm hero, why he was not re-elected in 1992. The fact is that the United States did in fact recover from the down wave much earlier than other nations. But also ask the Russians, the Japanese or even the French how they feel at present about 'new age economics'. For the rest of the world, the down wave is alive and well, but we would argue that it will soon follow the Anglo-American world out of the doldrums.

Why is the United States so far ahead of the crowd along the up wave? How has America not only escaped from the pitfalls of the 1990s, but also turned them into the longest peacetime expansion of the century? To put it more bluntly, how has our model of the long wave, described below, worked well for the rest of the world, especially Japan, but not completely for the United States? Who made it fail and turn awry 'locally'?

Part of the answer lies with Ronald Reagan, Art Laffer and their supply-side revolution which has taken time to bear fruit, but which is now deeply rooted in the American 'exception culturelle'.

But the main culprit is the only central banker who must have been aware that there was such thing as a long cycle and who must have read Irving Fisher's theories of 'debt-led crashes and depressions'. This man is Alan Greenspan and he deserves immense credit for immunizing the United States from the Japanese depression of the 1990s. What really singled him out initially was his ability to tackle the S&L crisis early in the decade. 'Hey, there is the rub!', for he then kept the United States away from the deflation plague, a lesson his Japanese counterpart should have learnt in his footsteps. But what has made Greenspan so unique in the last decade is the fact that he harboured no bias in fighting 'monetary disturbances', whether they stemmed from inflationary or deflationary threats.

He was therefore as keen to fight early hints of inflation in 1994 as he was quick to revert to anti-deflation moves throughout the Asian crisis, the Russian default and the LTCM bail out.[1] Other central bankers have consistently shown an anti-inflation bias, but only Greenspan seems to have steered halfway between these two antagonistic pitfalls of deflation and inflation. He recently confirmed his 'neutral bias' in the 22 July 1999 Humphrey Hawkins hearing, and in that sense he is a true disciple of Fisher.

In the 1930s, Fisher had claimed that depression was avoidable. In the 1990s, Greenspan proved it, as he cunningly managed to tame the long

---

[1] Long Term Capital Market, the famous hedge fund that came close to triggering the collapse of the world financial system in September 1998.

wave and have it work to the benefit of the United States, while the rest of the world was left to its reckless forces.

Thus, this book has two purposes: its first and primary goal is to tell the rest of the world that the worst is over and why. In so doing, we need to show how the long wave works: to this end, we present a model that borrows both from the Russian economist Nicolas Kondratieff and from Fisher, and 'breaks the wave' into three components: production, prices and debt. We shall elaborate on this below. The second purpose is to pay tribute to Greenspan, for whom we might have mixed feelings in a way. Above all, we remain impressed by the way he has handled US monetary policy since he was appointed Federal Reserve Chairman in August 1987. Incidentally, however, while he was taming the long wave, one could argue that he made our model less predictable or less true. In fact, what he tacitly suggested to us was that depressions were 'worst-case' scenarios within 'creative destruction' time periods, and that you could have creative destruction work for you. He needs a special tribute in this respect.

Thereafter, we will focus on our primary purpose, which deals essentially with the rest of the world, even if the special case of the United States constantly overshadows our arguments.

In fact, this book is both the extension and a positive version of an unpublished manuscript written at Easter 1989, which predicted *pêle-mêle* a Japanese crash, much more dangerous than that of October 1987, a universal real estate disaster, a banking crisis of unheard magnitude, a generalized recession and deflationary threats. At the time, what lay ahead of us was the last stage of the long down wave that had started in 1973, the very phase known as 'creative destruction' according to Joseph Schumpeter, with all the seeds of the following rebound, but whose negative side would be most spectacular:[2] a prolonged industrial recession, with its long list of banking and real estate bankruptcies, the threat of job obsolescence embedded in technological change and a tidal wave of de-localizations, triggering mounting unemployment and crawling deflation. In short, the Japanese syndrome!

---

[2] This was particularly true in Japan at the beginning of the 1990s and in Southeast Asia in 1997.

Many of these predictions were making the headlines as recently as October 1998, beginning with the wind of deflation that initially blew in from Southeast Asia[3] in the autumn of 1997 as a delayed echo of the great Japanese crisis of 1990 (the latter seemed to be reaching a climax in the winter of 1998). As late as 1996, Asia had been viewed as the future of the world, yet two years later it would threaten a downturn. Ambient pessimism was too excessive back then to be meaningful. How could we ignore the fact that the Asian crisis, however perturbing, was in fact instrumental in our logic of 'destructive creation', which is typical of the ultimate stage of the down wave? We clearly saw there a 'necessary purgatory', and the immediate prelude to the next ascending wave of the long cycle.

Thank you, Asia! Thank you for providing irrefutable evidence that we were living through the dying embers of a declining cycle, the end of a period of creative destruction, which finally purged the international financial system from an irrational and speculative debt binge. It was in Asia that the down wave found its epilogue. From then on, growth could again grip the world – Asia included.

Until recently, we could believe that the waning depression, of which Japan is the epicentre, was only a pale mirror image of events of the 1930s. Since its Asian manifestation, we knew that it was of comparable nature, if not really of the same width. In order to demonstrate this point, let us enumerate the causes of the Asian trauma of summer 1997. There were three of them:[4]

- Firstly, following in the footsteps of 1980s Japan, there was an obvious industrial and real estate over-investment, resulting in particular from excessive government incentives to stimulate supply and production, to the detriment of profitability.
- Secondly, the aggravation of external constraint: deterioration of competitiveness (in particular, through the rise of the US dollar), soaring current deficits and increased difficulties of external financing.

---

[3] Most notably Thailand, Malaysia, Indonesia, the Philippines and South Korea.

[4] We feel indebted here to our friend Guy Longueville, BNP's deputy chief economist, although the views expressed here are exclusively ours.

This led to the abandonment of the dollar peg in the most fragile countries: Thailand, Malaysia, the Philippines, Indonesia and, eventually, South Korea.

- Finally, the abandonment of the peg itself – a source of weakness for the heavily dollar-indebted local institutions – acted as a catalyst for a balance-sheet crisis.

It is especially this last aspect that made Asian jitters look like a delayed echo, albeit attenuated, of the Japanese crisis. The difference of scale between Asia and Japan, the recent positive moves of the latter, and the unconcealed impatience of some of the large US financial institutions to take over some ailing banks of the area underlined, however, in the winter of 1998/99, the temporary nature of the crisis.

In the short term, in fact, these countries are already benefiting from a fast recovery of their exports, stimulated by the depreciation of their currencies, and drawn both by US expansion and the European recovery. Moreover, objective economic complicity between them and the richer countries once again prevails. At one end of the spectrum, our populations are growing older while rich in capital and know-how, and at the other end, people are poor but younger, hard working, better and better trained, and eager to catch up with Western standards. This is why Asia-bound flows of capital very quickly resumed, at least in the form of direct investments, with certain Western companies regarding this crisis as a godsend.

In support of this view, the latest projections from the World Bank for Horizon 2020, published in June 1999, remain optimistic: 'On the whole, developing countries could record an average annual growth rate of between 5 per cent to 6 per cent per year from now to 2020 and see their share of world production double while passing from a sixth to a third. For the decade to come, developing countries' growth could reach 5.4 per cent per year against 2.6 per cent for the past decade.'

However, the very contenders of linear extrapolation, who in 1989 were heralding the unlimited continuation of the false prosperity of the 1980s – the 'insane years' – are even today retracting to a frightened stance. After being unable to visualize in time the accumulation of the storms that were going to violently rock the boat and get them lost in the fog and tempest without navigation instruments, how could they have possibly guessed that the Asian crisis was foreseeable, inevitable, salubrious and necessary? How could they now possess the right instinct of how to escape to safety?

With 25 years of study and practice of international equity strategy, this esoteric matter, at the border of economic science and portfolio management, allowed us to identify some pragmatic guidelines that are not integrated into the calculations of traditional economists. The latter tend to underestimate the contribution of Kondratieff's long wave theory, perhaps because it leaves little room for mathematical developments.

Long waves and short-term cycles: what is it all about?

The short-term cycle, sometimes called business cycle, can be defined as alternation over a three- to four-year span between expansion phases, which gradually degenerate into overheating, and recession intervals, which help the economy get rid of its excesses and put it on the road to recovery. These cycles usually coincide with the pulsation of political life: legislative or presidential elections.

On the contrary, the long cycle, sometimes called long wave, reflects the heavy trends[5] of economic life, which are undetectable to the naked eye: in terms of price, activity and debt. For the forecaster, the study of long cycles can be based on three strong observations:

•   First, it is a fact that economic history repeats itself, as far as its primary trends are concerned, approximately every 50 to 60 years. For example, the 1980s resemble a distant echo of the 1920s, with the combination in both cases[6] of a durable downtrend in prices, together with a rising upswing in debt accumulation.[7] Going back further in history,

---

[5] A major cycle can be broken down into two successive waves of 25 to 30 years each: an up wave and a down wave.

[6] Starting respectively in 1921 and 1981.

[7] The combination of disinflation and over-leverage is typical of a 'feel-good era' or false prosperity phase, which is the stuff of which financial bubbles are made: this 'insane years' syndrome was experienced in the 1920s on Wall Street and again in the 1980s in Japan. When the bubble bursts, a major crash develops, followed by a depression of the type Japan is still muddling through. The whole mechanism is described in detail in Chapter 6.

one finds a similar configuration in the years that followed the Battle of Waterloo (between 1815 and 1825) or the conclusion of the US Civil War (between 1865 and 1873). A further example of recurring 60-year anniversaries lies with the following sequence of major stock market crashes: London (1825), Vienna (1873), Wall Street (1929) and Tokyo (1990).

- Next, it should be stressed that these primary trends, once established, are there to last approximately one decade, so that they can be used as robust guidelines in order to help sort out daily random noises from the trend. Professional forecasters would be wrong to deprive themselves of their help.

  To give an example: at the beginning of 1994, world interest rates went up strongly for nine months, leaving the markets perplexed. Within this context, the contenders of long cycles were able to advocate that the powerful wave of disinflation that had started in 1981, and was in essence favourable to the relaxation of interest rates, had not come to an end. Hence, one was confronted with a significant deviation above trend, but this was provisional. Indeed, the regression to the mean acted as a violent backlash from November 1994 and through the whole of 1995, ie. rates again dropped back severely.

- Admittedly, the precision of this repetitive mechanism does not apparently match the rigour of the laws of astronomy, and the major inflection points which mark the transition from one trend to the next can be more or less manipulated, at least managed, by human intervention: we refer here to the interaction between long and short cycles, the latter being easier to handle. We will elaborate on this in connection with the Gulf crisis, where 'an invisible hand', a US hand in fact, precipitated the Japanese crash.

The story that we now tell and the good news that we intend to impart are thus largely founded on the theories of long cycles named after Kondratieff, a brilliant Russian economist who established them in 1925, and who died, deported to Siberia, in 1938.

What is pointed out here, and which should be obvious to all, is that the industrial world had experienced structural downturns in the late 19th century and in the 1930s comparable to what has occurred since the oil crisis of 1973; each time, when the conditions were met and their causes cleaned up,[8] the world rebounded – for 30 years.

To familiarize the reader with these theories and their associated vocabulary, we propose a preliminary excursion into the universe of cycles via our section 'The Marvellous Clock'.

In Chapter 1 Kondratieff presents his long price cycle, with price fluctuations being the core of the theory and its only statistically validated piece. However, we tentatively add two components to this theory: one on debt, drawn from Fisher's debt deflation model of 1933;[9] the other on growth, or production, borrowed from the 1959 doctorate thesis of Gaston Imbert.[10]

These theories are developed in Chapter 2. In brief, on both sides of a bell-shaped price chart viewed as central, we visualize two additional and identical waves: a production (or growth) wave, supposed to lead prices; and a debt wave, viewed as a delayed echo of inflation. We thus formally present a long wave model, both stylized and original, putting together three parameters: production, prices and debt, and synthesizing the works of Kondratieff, Fisher and Imbert.

A chart can be said to be worth 1000 words. Hence, it is a chart that we place at the forefront of our explanation (see Figure 1), enabling us to identify and clearly isolate the various phases of a complete long cycle.

In Chapter 3, we put the model to the test through the prism of history, using a double approach: chronological and thematic. The latter opens with a cross-sectional presentation, where each typical phase of the long cycle is illustrated with a table. Each table is representative of one of five themes, namely: previous up wave, stagflation time, bubble years leading to a debt induced stock crash, depression and golden age. Each theme is then illustrated in two ways: first, by an array of chronological references which characterize it (eg. 1920 to 1929), and second, by the nicknames which history books attach to these episodes (eg. 'the American house of cards' or 'insane years').

---

[8] Inflation and over-indebtedness.

[9] Fisher, I.: 'The debt deflation theory of great depressions', Econometrica (1933).

[10] Imbert, G.: 'Des mouvements de longue durée Kondratieff', Aix-en-Provence (1959).

Chronologically, we demonstrate how the 'marvellous clock' perfectly describes the three preceding cycles of capitalism to World War II, the latter marking, in an unusual way, the border between the third and fourth major cycle. Until then, major wars had been associated with the peaks of cycles, such as World War I, the Franco-Prussian War of 1870, the US Civil War and the Napoleonic wars. They were thus located in the midst of the long cycle,[11] and not at the hinge between two cycles. Contrary to this scheme, and through the massive destructions it entailed, World War II prolonged the depression phase of the 1930s. At the same time, it contributed to the rise of the US production machine, which was already on a recovery path at the eve of the war. Bloodier than any other, it helped to work out the political configuration of the world until the fall of the Berlin Wall in 1989.

More destructive than any other, it did, however, open the way to the ensuing three 'miracle decades' of the post-war era. In that sense, this conflict really embodied the concept of 'creative destruction' typical of the transition periods which herald the ascending phase of the next major cycle.

And so this brings us to our second section, entitled 'The Magnificent Parallel', and to our central demonstration: that is, if the 'miracle years' of 1945 to 1973 easily qualify as the ascending wave of the fourth Kondratieff cycle, are we in the last moments of the downturn of that cycle? Or, in other words, does the period 1973 to 1997 fit the down wave model such as is described by us in its various phases?[12]

If such is the case, then it must follow, as night the day, that the next ascending wave is not far.

Here we touch upon the raison d'être of this book, which is to warn the 'rest of the world' about the forthcoming radical and positive changes in economic conditions that will soon be experienced in the wake of the United States. Incidentally, the Anglo-American world should continue to surf on the 'goldilocks' wave for a while longer, indeed much longer.

This is why we submit the long crisis that began in 1973 to spectral analysis along the lines suggested in Chapter 2. This analysis awakens a

---

[11] The Vietnam War also satisfies this criterion.

[12] Stagflation, false prosperity (financial bubble), major crash and depression.

strong feeling of déjà vu and allows us to establish an undeniable parallel between the two periods 1913 to 1937 and 1973 to 1997.

This 'magnificent parallel' is defined in four steps.[13] Each one is dedicated to a precise phase of the down wave: comparison between the 1910s and the 1970s, or illustration of the 'stagflation' concept; mimicry between the 1920s and the 1980s, or the 'financial bubble' syndrome; similarity between Tokyo 1990 and Wall Street 1929, the twinned archetypes of a debt-induced stock market crash; and finally, the amazing resemblance between the 1930s and the 1990s, or the mysteries of the final phase of the crisis.

Here, we are at the heart of our argument. We stress two major reasons to justify our optimism:

- Following Fisher's footsteps, inflation and over-leverage are the two evils hampering growth. When these causes are 'cleaned up', which is largely the case today in the United States and in Europe, the extension of the crisis does not have a raison d'être any more, other than its own inertia.

- The final phase of the crisis, or 'depression', of the kind we still currently experience in Japan, Russia and to a lesser extent Asia, is always double-faced: the first one reflects the destructive effects of the clean up of leverage excess of the preceding phase, which ends up in a major banking crisis and a collapse of credit and business; the other, renamed 'creative destruction', bears the seeds of the rebound of the next up wave, namely the ongoing technological and sociological revolution,[14] as well as the potential extension of industrial development to new areas.[15]

---

[13] In fact, chapters.

[14] Kondratieff recalls that 'the up wave of the first cycle took off with the Industrial Revolution amidst deep changes in the production process affecting . . . all major industrial branches: textile mills, chemicals, metallurgy and others . . .'. He stresses that this revolution was an outgrowth of a wave of technological change that could be traced back to the 1764–1795 time frame. As for the beginning of the up wave of the second cycle, the Russian economist gives further details, referring to 'a major improvement in the steam engine (1824), the invention of the turbine (1824 to 1827), . . . Portland cement (1824), . . . the first automobile (1831), . . . the first harvesting machine (1831), . . . telegraph (1832), . . . the first steam boat (1836),

This final phase is truly the prelude to the upswing of the next major cycle. This is where we will, from then on, focus our projector. We shall devote our third section to it. It will be the final touch to our efforts.

'Every cloud has a silver lining' becomes our motto, following in Countess de Ségur's footsteps,[16] a remote echo of the Latin proverb that any stockbroker at least should endorse: 'Sperat adversis timuit secundis alteram sortem bene preparatum pectus'.[17]

This is where we show how our down wave is waning, bearing with it the seeds of revival.

There is a Chinese ideogram that expresses the concepts of both 'crisis' and 'opportunity'. The extraordinary chaotic fruitfulness of the depression phase that we have gone through, in particular in Japan and in Europe since 1990 and for the last two years in Asia, has followed the same pattern of destructive creation. This duality applies to the painful process of credit and asset deflation, whose purpose is to clean the system of its excess leverage, to erase the wrongdoings of the past and to set out again on a healthier basis: it signifies the return to an equity culture as opposed to a leverage culture. By the same token, the excesses of the welfare state are leaving room for the solutions of supply-side economics. The challenge of technological change, although initially leading to huge lay-offs in older industries, finally opens access to a 'new frontier', with infinite virtual space and 'green digitized pastures',[18] a remote echo of the Conquest of the West.

. . . rotative press (1846), etc . . .'. For the third cycle's up wave, Kondratieff mentions especially 'Gramme's continuous current dynamo (1870), the telephone (1877), Siemens' electric locomotive (1878), nitric acid (1880), the petrol engine (1885), the diesel engine (1893) and airplanes (1895)'.

[15] This criterion is used by Kondratieff to qualify the beginning of a new up wave, when the club of developed countries extends to a set of newly industrialized areas: the United States around 1840, Australia, Canada, Argentina and Chile around 1890. Kondratieff might have mentioned Tsarist Russia but abstains for obvious reasons.

[16] A Russian-born French writer, one of whose best known novels is entitled *Après la pluie, le beau temps*.

[17] Literally, 'a well-prepared heart will anticipate the reversals of fortune: it keeps hoping in adversity, while remaining cool-headed in good times'.

[18] If we may use this tribute to US Western mythology.

Maybe everyone will be able to set up their virtual ranch there, capitalizing on their creative know-how and expertise in a gushing and bustling environment prone to profitable planetary exchanges?

To conclude, in the closing chapter we recapitulate, by classifying them, all the obvious signs that the crisis is ending. The non-exhaustive inventory of reasons for hope, which we present at this level, has surprised even ourselves, both from a technological standpoint and from the more market-oriented signs that we singled out – the United States playing a precursory part there.

In fact, if anything, the United States must not only be singled out here as a harbinger of things to come elsewhere, but also as a provocative anomaly with respect to our model. For how is it that America escaped in style 'the pangs of despised love, the oppressor's wrong, the proud man's contumely, the law's delay, the insolence of office, and the spurns that patient merit of the unworthy takes' that are usually associated with the last stage of a down wave? The answer is that someone managed to immunize the United States from the 1930s-type depression that Japan went through. Maybe for the first time in history, long waves have encountered their master – Alan Greenspan.

Rightly or wrongly, we have mixed feelings about this. For, at the very time when we thought we had unveiled some of the best kept secrets of long wave theory, someone else had probably reached the same conclusions; but as Federal Reserve Chairman, he also had the power to change the course of history. By doing it, he confused our own findings, at least partially. Fortunately, most other central bankers were not as smart as he, allowing our model to keep some credibility. *'Foul is fair and fair is foul'* (Macbeth).

Lastly, for impassioned economists and stock market strategists, we introduce an empirical and stylized model of the business cycle published in 1981 in the *Revue d'Economie Politique* and whose potential synergies with our long model appear most profitable.

PART ONE

THE MARVELLOUS CLOCK

The Marvellous Clock

The long cycle is to the business cycle in the economic world what the small hand is to the big hand in the measurement of time: its movement is invisible to the naked eye.

Four major cycles have been completed, or almost completed, since the appearance of industrial capitalism at the end of the 18th century. Their periodicity does not have the regularity of a Swiss clock, nor even of a countryside cuckoo clock, but it stems from a more complex determinism, which remains clock related. To better visualize the difference that separates them, let us say that a usual clock complies with its time schedule, while Kondratieff's pendulum fares much better: it sets appointments and meets them.

From the point of view of the cycle, three essential questions are raised: production (quantities), distribution or rationing (prices), and transfers across time (debt). To focus, as Kondratieff did, on the evolution over time of any of these three parameters, also means to be interested in both of the others. But it also raises the age wave problem, with its underlying conflict of generations,[19] which brings us to an analysis of demographic cycles. In a word, when the youngest generations are numerically dominant, they impose inflationary policies, supporting consumption and real estate to the detriment of saving and financial assets, at least until an inflationary crisis of the 1920 or 1980 type occurs. When these same age groups grow older, their voting power imposes on the economic authorities a complete policy reversal, this time supporting increased saving incentives to the benefit of financial assets, and to the detriment of consumption and real estate.

This attitude makes it possible to rebuild the stock of capital that will feed the ascending wave of the ensuing long cycle.

---

[19] The age wave feud.

Long wave followers, such as Michel Lutfalla and Jacques Marseille in France, Ed Hyman and Ed Yardeni in the United States, and Manfred Neumann in Germany, have worked on these phenomena,[20] which they have described at length.

If the analysis of long-term price fluctuations, upon which we will linger, remains the kernel of the long wave theory, this theory would not be complete without the introduction into the model of the two other parameters mentioned above: production[21] (growth) and debt. We claim this as our most important contribution.

For it is precisely the interactions between these three variables, and, more exactly, the sequence of leads and lags that they follow in a well-regulated ballet, which make sure our 'marvellous clock' will be able to honour its appointments at very precise landmarks of a choreography immutable in space if not completely faithful in time.

This 'space' is the imaginary landscape of peaks, plateaus and valleys, which we will describe now: production peak, inflation crest, plateau of activity, mountain of debt, valley of depression and slope of recovery.

Applied to the period that we have lived through since 1945, the phases of the long cycle are shown in Figure 1.

We shall now explain the origin of these phases.

---

[20] Neumann, M.: 'The rise and fall of the wealth of nations, long waves in economics and international politics', Edward Elgar, Cheltenham (1997).

[21] It is within Imbert's 1959 Aix-en-Provence thesis on long wave theory that we initially found the first arguments for a built-in lag between prices and production. However, it is in Fisher's 1933 analysis of the US debt recession that the idea came out of the primary role of indebtedness in the genesis of long cycles.

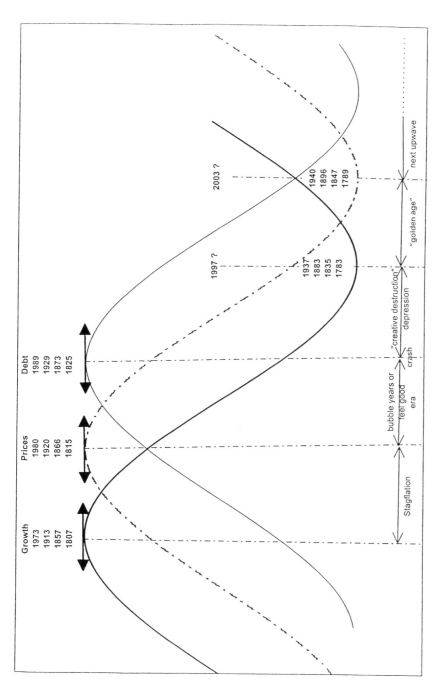

Figure 1. *The 'marvellous clock', or the subsequent phases of Kondratieff's long waves of production, prices and debt*

1

The Theory of the Long Cycle

The idea that economic phenomena proceed primarily by alternation of phases of expansion and contraction is not new. Much research has been devoted to the concept, of which the most recent can be broken down into two schools of thought. The first extends from 1923 to 1947, with the work of Kondratieff, De Wolff, Schumpeter, Cassel and Dupriez. The second starts at the beginning of the 1970s with studies by Forrester, Mandel, Monsch and Van Duijn. The most widely known cycles are:

The seasonal movement	12 months
Kitchin's cycle	3 to 4 years
Juglar's cycle	6 to 8 years
Kuznets' cycle	22 to 23 years
Kondratieff's cycle	50 to 60 years

Let us remember here that Kitchin's cycle corresponds to the definition of the US business cycle whose periodicity is dictated by the presidential election cycle. Long wave analysis started with the statistical observation of the time series of wholesale prices going back to 1760. It led to the discovery of the alternation of long phases of expansion and contraction of prices by Kondratieff.

The price cycle

On the basis of the statistical observation of the time series of wholesale prices, Kondratieff put forth the assumption in 1925 that three successive major inflation cycles[22] could be identified.

---

[22] Kondratieff, N.D.: 'Les grands cycles de la conjoncture', Economica, Paris, 1992, pp 118–119.

The rising phase of the first cycle takes in the period of 1789 to 1814, ie. 25 years. The downward wave of the first cycle starts in 1814 and ends in 1849 and thus lasts 35 years. The entire cycle in the movement of prices is completed in 60 years.

The rising wave of the second cycle begins in 1849 and ends in 1873, 24 years later. True, for the United States the prices peak in 1866, but this can be explained by the Civil War. The observed lack of coincidence between the turning point for prices in the United States, on the one hand, and for England and France, on the other, does not invalidate the overall picture of the development of the cycle. The downward phase of the second cycle starts in 1873 and finishes in 1896, thus lasting 23 years. The entire second cycle is completed in 47 years.

The ascending wave of the third cycle starts in 1896 and finishes in 1920, thus lasting 24 years. According to all available data, the downward wave of the third cycle began in 1920. Thus, in the movement of the average price level since the 1780s, we can distinguish two and a half long cycles. They are not of the same length, since they range from 47 to 60 years, the first cycle being the longest.

Kondratieff's main contribution is to have given the world these groundbreaking concepts that form the basis of long wave theory. Four major Kondratieff cycles, made of the symmetrical alternation of inflation and disinflation waves, have been recognized ever since. By symmetrical, we mean the fact that the duration of the up wave is about equal to that of the down wave.

	Inflation	Disinflation
Kondratieff I	1789–1814	1815–1847
Kondratieff II	1847–1866	1867–1896
Kondratieff III	1897–1920	1921–1940
Kondratieff IV	1940–1980	1981–?

This symmetry leads us to project a bell-shaped curve for the graphical representation of these waves, which is best illustrated by the trend of the US year-to-year retail price index from 1960 to date. Indeed, the resulting graph, with its sine-curve profile, empirically validates Kondratieff's

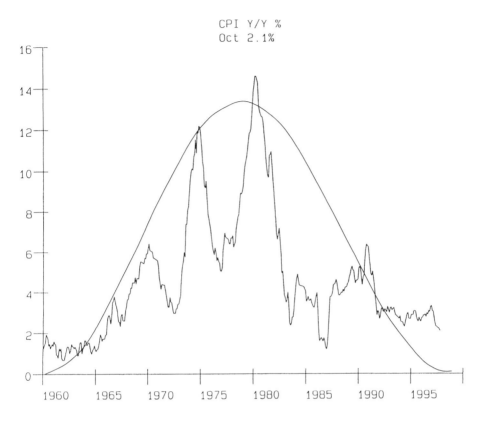

CPI Y/Y %
Oct 2.1%

Figure 2. *Evolution of the rate of inflation in the United States from 1960 to 1997 (year-to-year variations)*

Source: Ed Hyman, International Strategy & Investment

theory for a period posterior to his work (see Figure 2). Indeed, one finds this very silhouette in the Russian economist's original paper on the price chart of the French 'rente',[23] which is the mirror image of interest rates. It clearly reveals two complete long cycles (see Figure 3).

Let us remember that the price of the rente rises when long–term rates fall and vice versa. On the basis of a top in rates in 1815 (and thus of a bottom for the rente), the primary trend is clearly one of falling

---

[23] The French 'rente' was a perpetuity yielding 3 per cent per year with a 100 francs face value. Whenever market rates rose above 3 per cent, the rente price fell below par. Conversely, if market rates fell below 3 per cent, the rente was priced above par.

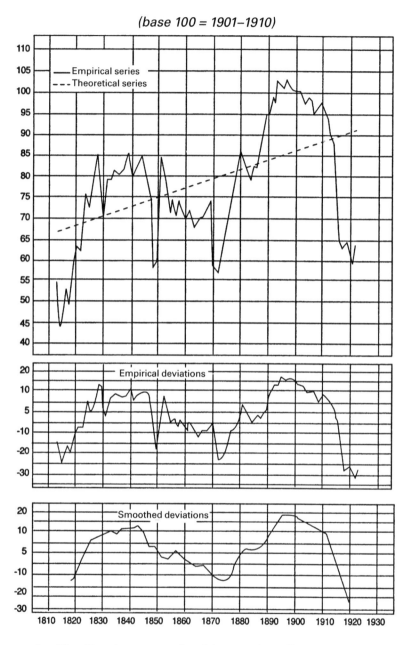

Figure 3. *The French rente analysed by Kondratieff in the period 1815 to 1922*

Source: Original Kondratieff article in *Review of Economic Statistics*, November 1935.

rates until 1850, at least if one disregards two major incidents: the fall of French king Charles X in 1830 and that of his successor Louis Philippe in 1848. Between 1850 and 1866 rates are on the rise for economic reasons as the up wave matures. From 1866 onwards, long rates are on their way down, as inflation abates both in England and in the United States in the aftermath of the Civil War, at least until the collapse of Imperial France at the battle of Sedan. For the third time in 40 years, the fall of the French rente for political reasons interferes with economic logic. Very quickly, however, this logic prevails again with a vengeance, and the rente rises sharply from 1873 until 1896. From 1896 to 1913, the rente price consolidates gently, despite a steady rise in interest rates. The war of 1914 and the subsequent inflationary push that it triggers will accelerate its fall until 1920.

The production cycle

If, instead of focusing on the long-term trend of prices, we now concentrate on the fluctuations of production, the symmetry between up waves and down waves appears to lose its substance.

Whereas the long-term price cycle is completely symmetrical, justifying its chart representation by a bell-shaped curve, the parallel observation of a production index (or business activity index) does not seemingly present this symmetry (see Figure 4). Each complete cycle is in fact made of an alternation of three different phases: expansion, plateau and depression.

The plateau phase, which is a long period of stagnation or weak growth, breaks itself up into two halves of approximately ten years each: stagflation (P1), marked by the combined effects of slower growth and rising inflation, and the feel-good era (P2), associated with the beginning of disinflation and a rising debt wave – an ideal combination to feed a financial bubble. The latter, while leading to a major crash, ends up in a depression.

However, if we want production to unfold in a sinusoidal pattern, suffice it to express its variations, not in absolute terms, but rather in derivative form, ie. in terms of growth.

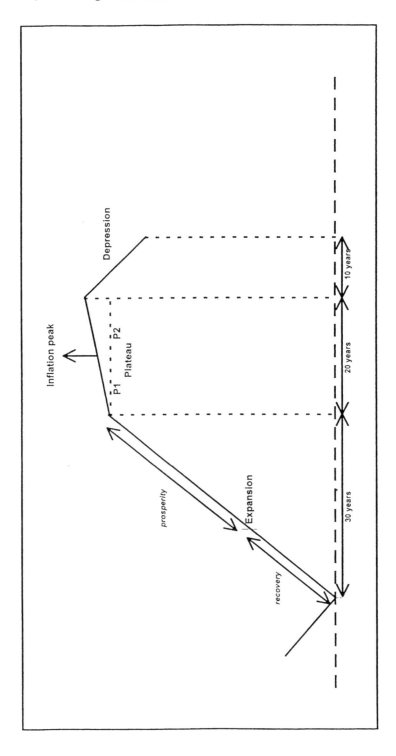

Figure 4. *The quantity cycle: a stylized production index*

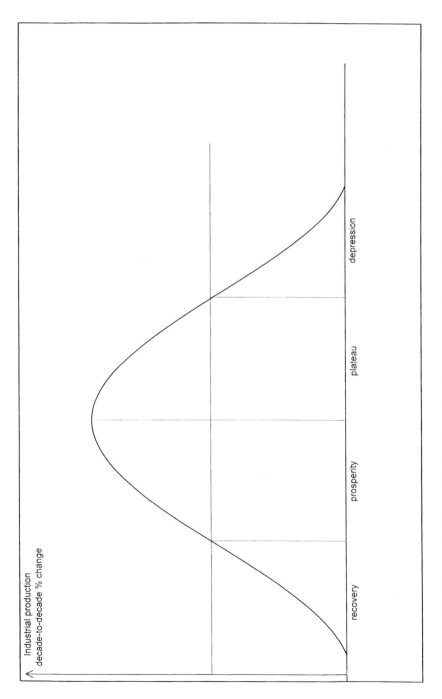

Figure 5. *The production cycle: decade-to-decade percentage change of the annual industrial production index*

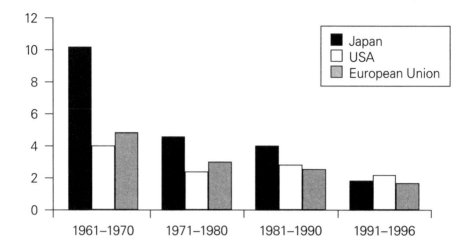

Figure 6. *GDP Growth rates: US, Europe, Japan*

Source: EUROSTAT/DG II Commission européenne.

Let us present, in a stylized way, the percentage change of industrial production not on a year-to-year basis but on a decade-to-decade basis: ie. one compares the annual indices of industrial production at ten-year intervals.

Generalizing in the long run our approach to the business cycle, we observe that the series thus obtained graphically fits a bell-shaped curve of the type shown in Figure 5.

If we live through a Kondratieff cycle, we have to accept the idea that a down wave is possible. A concrete illustration of the production down wave that started in the 1970s can be viewed in Figure 6.

This representation in terms of business momentum enables us to formulate, in a familiar form, the main phases of the production cycle:

- The 30-year period of positive momentum (up wave) that covers the phases of recovery and prosperity: ie. the post-war miracle years of 1945 to 1973.
- The 30-year period of negative momentum (down wave) covers two distinct phases:
    - The *plateau*, extending on a couple of decades and marked by a clear growth slowdown such as in the period 1973 to 1989.

– *Depression* itself, finally, which starts with the implosion of a financial bubble and the first signs of debt deflation, eg. the Russian and Japanese depressions, together with the European stagnation of the 1990s.

This illustration leads us to formulate the following proposition: in terms of decennial rate of change, the stylized evolution of the production cycle is similar to the price cycle: it follows the same bell-shaped pattern, with identical periodicity, but with a lag.

The reader should take note of this lag: we will justify it in due course. Let us elaborate first on the three phases.

Expansion (up wave)

The expansion phase extends over approximately 30 years and comprises two parts: a 'golden age' recovery of 5 to 10 years from the preceding depression and a period of prosperity beyond.

It is generally triggered by a new technical revolution leading to industrial applications (such as the steam engine, the railway, the automobile, electric power and data processing). That the basic business trend should remain upward for 25 to 30 years does not preclude fluctuations of the business cycle around this trend, with an alternation of expansion and recession phases. However, during this 30-year prosperity period, the expansion phases of the business cycle are appreciably longer than the interludes of recession that alternate with them. Conversely, during the era of depression, the stagnation or recession phases of the business cycle are longer than those of recovery.[24]

To provide two historical examples of what an up wave looks like:

• Coming out of the depression of 1873 to 1883, the period 1883 to 1913 remained in history as La Belle Epoque, because of the outstanding improvements to the living standards of the average person which it brought in: the railroad, the automobile, electric

---

[24] As suggested by the economist Spiethoff, quoted in Kondratieff, N.D.: 'Les grands cycles de la conjoncture', Economica, Paris, 1992, p 148

power and so forth. It should be noted that the revival of activity that took off in 1883 was sustained for ten years together with a continuation of the price deflation of the previous decade, with the bottom of the price wave being earmarked for the middle of the 1890s. Here comes the lag again, which forms the basis for the model that we shall propose below! Indeed, the coincidence of a resumption of production and a continuation of disinflation made this a period of success, a paradise for rentiers and shareholders, at least until 1913. A similar lag is perfectly observable today in the United States, a country with a strong lead in the world cycle, allowing its rentiers and shareholders, as well as their workers, to also enjoy their golden age.

- Closer to us in time, the period 1945 to 1973, often called the post-World War II 'miracle years', was marked by the assertion of US supremacy as well as by the economic rebirth of the two great losers of World War II: Germany and Japan.

Plateau (early down wave)

The plateau phase extends on a couple of decades and is marked by a degree of structural production slowdown compared with the previous successful era.

Let us recall, as noted previously, that the plateau phase breaks up into two halves, of which one is strongly inflationary (eg. 1910 to 1920 or 1970 to 1980) and the second, falsely prosperous and characterized by a financial bubble (1920 to 1929 or 1980 to 1989). The bursting of the financial bubble through a spectacular crash marks the end of the plateau and entry into depression. It is mainly because the similarities were striking between the 1920s and the 1980s, then again between the 1930s and the 1990s, that the idea of this book became so compelling to us.

Depression or creative destruction (late down wave)

The depression phase, while most often representative of a whole decade, usually extends only over a period from five to seven years. It can be best described as a transition period between the old cycle and the new one. It is the time when new technologies are displacing the old ones.

Thus, it is destructive on the one hand as it stresses job obsolescence in lots of areas of the old economy; but it also bears the seeds of revival.

It begins following a stock market crash of world proportions, which puts an end to the debt-fuelled speculation of the preceding phase. The crash is an asset deflation phenomenon. This asset deflation unfolds in tandem with a debt deflation, which weakens the banking system and deprives the central bank of its usual relays for monetary creation, with extremely negative effects on the real economy. The Great Depression of the 1930s is the best known example of such a dreadful spiral, because it is still very much alive in most memories, but the situation which Japan currently lives through, and, to a lesser extent, until recently experienced by the Eurozone and Southeast Asian countries, is to all intents and purposes very similar to this period.

We shall reconsider the concept of depression in Chapter 8 as 'worst case scenario of destructive creation periods'.

The long wave and the life cycle

One of the keys to the long price cycle is the age wave phenomenon. By this we mean that the relative weight of the younger generations compared to the declining age classes is itself cyclical. When the 'yuppie-to-nerd ratio' is high and rising, the numerically dominant class tends to impose pro-growth and pro-inflation policies. Think of the 'baby boomers' of the 1960s and 1970s, whose major concern at the time was to acquire real assets (housing) and to fight for their wage purchasing power. Twenty years later, these same categories, now 'papy boomers' have joined the rentiers' camp. But, as they remain numerically dominant, this time they impose restrictive monetary and budgetary policies. Is it pure chance if the peak of inflation in the United States coincided with the roll-over of the age wave, or with the beginning of the papy-boom era? To understand this versatility of attitudes, we call upon the observation of the life cycle, which we draw from Merton Miller's 1972 course in macroeconomics at the University of Chicago Graduate School of Business.

This illustration of the three ages of life demonstrates the two successive behaviours of individuals.

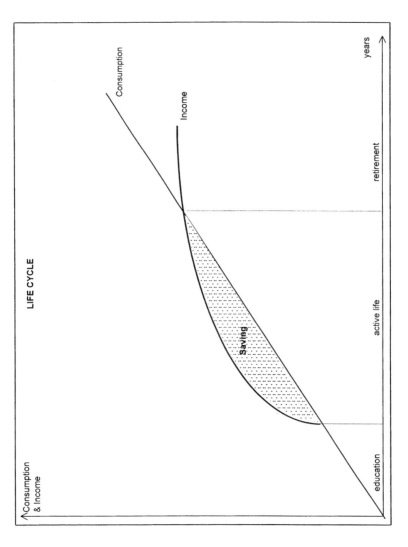

Figure 7. *The life cycle*

Source: extract from Upton and Miller's *Macroeconomy: a neoclassical approach*, University of Chicago Press, 1972

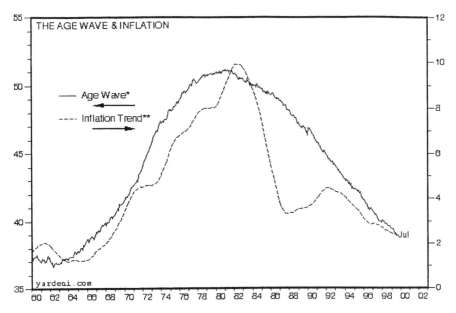

* Percent of labour force 16–34 years old.
** Five year moving average of yearly percent change in GPI

Figure 8. *Inflation and the age wave in the United States*

Source: Ed Yardeni, Deutsche Morgan Grenfell

As net debtors for the first 30 years, they benefit from inflation to constitute an estate and indulge in a consumption binge; becoming net creditors thereafter, they wish for the return of disinflation to preserve the purchasing power of their financial assets. This duality expresses a new type of conflict of generations, therefore of age classes of which the depression would mark the climactic form. This traditional type of conflict between the younger and older generations is also a social reflection of more stereotyped cleavages: between the 'haves' and the 'have nots', between the public and private sectors, between the rentiers and the unemployed. Is it a coincidence if the life cycle, and its conflicting economic logic, can be viewed as underlying the secular impulses that agitate the world macro-economy? Is it pure chance that the French Revolution of 1789 appeared at the bottom of a price wave and in the early years of a production up wave? The same can be said for the Revolution of 1848, some 59 years later, and what about the fall of the Berlin Wall in the 1989 ailing Soviet Union?

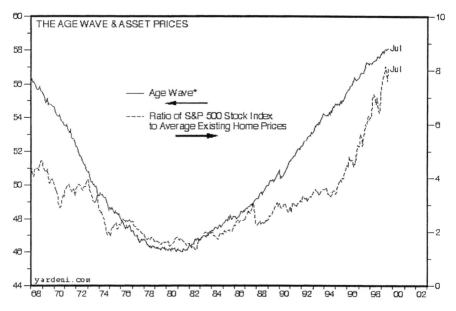

* Percent of labour force 35–64 years old.

Figure 9. *The age wave and asset arbitration in the United States*
Source: Ed Yardeni, Deutsche Morgan Grenfell

However, we must return to less political and more economic discussion. It is no coincidence if the inflation peak of 1980 occurred at a time when the US labour force started greying. In contrast, the inflation up wave seems to have gone hand in hand with the rejuvenating phase of the labour force. More generally, and with the lags that we have underlined, the ascending phase of any Kondratieff cycle would need to be carried by a new up wave of the demographic cycle.

The relative ageing of the US working population in the 1980s induced a decline in the relative weight of real estate in household assets and a corresponding rise in the proportion of their financial assets.

Consequently, how should we reconcile our hope that the richer countries are bound for their next economic up wave with the scheduled ageing of their populations? The answer is due to the fact that every new major cycle acts as a 'promoter of emergence' for poor countries. However, this time, the newcomers are both numerically heavier (China, India, Indonesia, Latin America etc) and structurally younger people than those of the Group of Seven (G7). Thus they will instantaneously rejuvenate the demographic profile of all players on the chessboard of the world economy.

Once again, thank you, Asia! Their speculative bubble has now been cleaned up, while their demographic wave is set to spur world growth.

2
Modelling the Relationships Between Production, Prices and Debt: A Long Wave Approach

We are beginning to feel as though we ourselves may be living through a Kondratieff wave that began roughly in 1945. It is necessary for us to explore this idea further until promoting the case convincingly.

The lag between prices and production

There is often a misunderstanding in current language between the price cycle and the quantity cycle. The best example of language abuse one can find in this field is the confusion, often maintained by the financial newspapers themselves, between the concepts of depression and deflation. Yet, the word depression refers to a long period of stagnation or contraction of production, while deflation applies to a phase of structural contraction of prices. In the same way, some ill-informed observers naturally tend to assimilate any production up wave with a corresponding price up wave. Nothing is more counter-intuitive, however, than this widespread confusion. Indeed, as the supply-siders like to claim, 'When there is a bumper crop of apples, what happens to the price of apples?' In a word, abundance is in itself rather deflationary: let us refer for instance to the growing flood of cheap products from Asia.[25] Conversely, a

---

[25] And whose quality is comparable to those of the older countries, especially within their mid-range and mass production niches.

dynamics of scarcity is inflationary: as soon as any product becomes rare, it becomes expensive. Consequently, if one admits the existence of a price cycle and simultaneously of a quantity cycle, nothing would make us think that they are constantly 'in sync' – quite the opposite in fact.

This observation is so well founded that the Kondratieff statisticians are divided into two camps: one for the dating of quantities (group 1) and the other for the dating of prices (group 2). This dichotomy is summarized perfectly in a table drawn from the Bulletin of Belgium General Bank of February 1988, where it is shown that production systematically leads prices as equally on the way up as on the way down.

The leadership of quantities (production) versus prices has received the theoretical support of many authors, notably Joshua Goldstein in the United States and Manfred Neumann, in his latest work on the long cycle.[26]

The latter connects 'the phases of growth and decline of the economy and the alternation of hard working bee-type generations, followed by welfare-prone and *cicadas*-type age classes'. In Neumann's opinion, 'the fluctuations of real activity are the leading factor'. It is due to investment – through which innovation is actually implemented and materialized – being added to consumption, that prices and interest rates eventually, after a lag, must follow volume growth on the way up. This last proposal, in particular, echoes our own thinking on the relationship between the long wave and the life cycle.

Thus we are confronted once again with this famous lag, which kept cropping up in Chapter 1.

The peak of inflation halfway through the production plateau

Let us first try and estimate the duration of this lag. Our assumption is that the top of the price cycle is halfway through the production plateau, ie. a lag of an eighth of a period. For a 56-year period, the lag would

---

[26] Neumann, M.: 'The rise and fall of the wealth of nations, long waves in economics and international politics', Edward Elgar, Cheltenham (1997).

thus be approximately seven years. Let us stress this point again: quantities lead prices or prices lag quantities. We shall now try and justify this lag on a theoretical basis before subjecting it to the test of experience.

It is natural to see the industrial apogee (ie. the peak of growth) precede the top in prices: when growth decelerates, the problems of income and wealth distribution will create or accelerate a dynamics of scarcity. We also note this same phenomenon for the business cycle. However, this logic of scarcity is not the immediate cause for the throttling of activity, neither in the case of the short cycle, nor in the case of the long cycle. In the case of the short cycle, it is the accelerating rise in interest rates, and their levelling off, which makes the cycle slide into recession. In the case of the long cycle, it is the tide of debt and debt-fuelled financial speculation that lead to a crash and to the onset of depression thereafter. However, one does not move brutally from a state of hyperinflation into depression. There must be a transition stage, fed by the first signs of disinflation. Consequently, the inflation peak is located somewhere along the plateau, between the production peak and the edge of depression.

To simplify matters, we will assume that it is located halfway across the plateau phase, thus dividing it into two contrasted halves:

- The first half is characterized by accelerating inflation, such as that between 1913 and 1920 or between 1973 and 1980.
- The second half is marked by the beginning of disinflation, creating a financial euphoria, and hence the name of 'feel-good era', such as that between 1920 and 1929.

In (1) (see Fig. 10), we see the last stage of price deflation (bottom price graph), which generally accompanies the first signs of renewed activity: the golden age. In (2), we see the period when prosperity (upper production graph) and prices (bottom graph) rise in tandem: maturing prosperity. In (3), we see the first half of the production plateau phase (top graph) corresponding to the period of hyperinflation (lower graph): stagflation. In (4), we see the feel-good era, which is the second half of the plateau, and which combines both the final bursts of volume growth (top graph), with the first signs of disinflation following the inflation peak (lower graph). In (5), we see the slump in production that accompanies price deflation: depression at work, as in today's Japan.

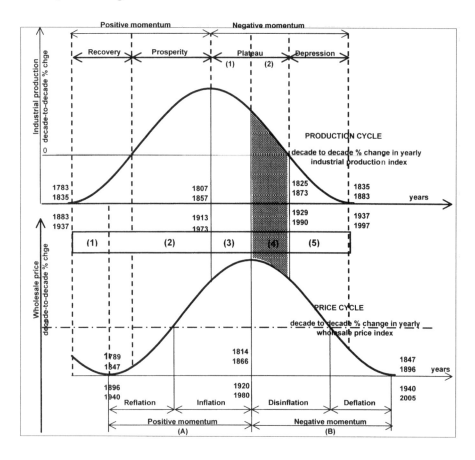

Figure 10. *The lag between price and production cycles*

Identification of the feel-good era or speculative prosperity

The first of the two halves of the production plateau is clearly defined: to the west by the production peak and to the east by the peak in prices. The period from 1973 to 1980 is a recent example of this. However, it

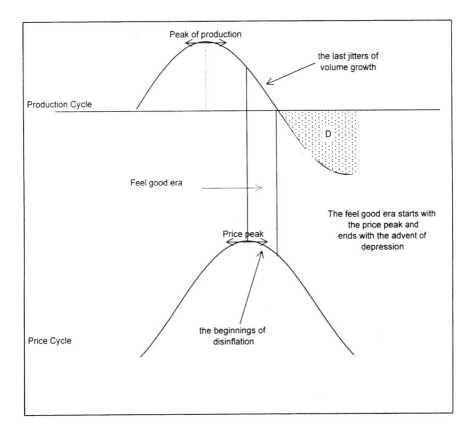

Figure 11. *The feel-good era between the price peak and the crater of depression*

is the second half that is of greatest interest, since it is the prelude to depression. Let us try and define its nature in order to better identify it. Note, first of all, that since it is bounded on the west by the price peak and on the east by the crater of depression, it combines the final bursts of volume growth with the early signs of price disinflation. This so-called feel-good era is thus clearly identified within our model of the relationship between prices and production, as shown in Figure 11.

However, in practical terms, with the extent of the depression contours remaining unspecified, we are in search of a more precise eastern marker to our plateau. This is where the mountain of debt comes into play.

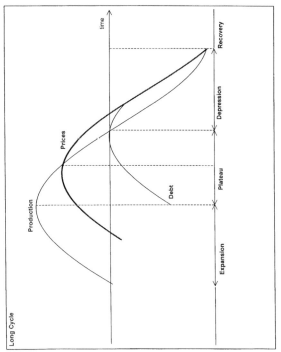

Model of the long cycle (debt)
(56 years)

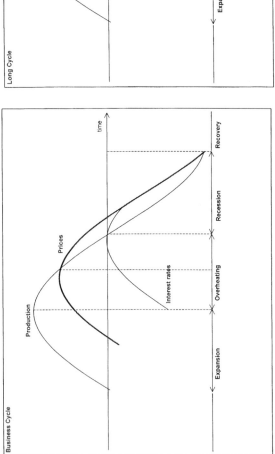

Model of the short cycle (interest rate)
(4 years)

Figure 12. Analogies between the business cycle and the long cycle

Introduction of the debt cycle: Irving Fisher's model

If we borrow Fisher's definition whereby the onset of the depression coincides with the debt peak, we can apply our short-term model of the relationship between production, prices and interest rates to the long term.

This time, the relationship applies to production, prices and debt, with the same pattern and time lags except for the time scale.[27] In this context, the peak in rates is to the business cycle what the peak of debt is to the long cycle: a prime signal of the economy entering recession (respectively, depression).

If we focus on the long cycle, the significance of this lead and lag pattern is as follows:

- Phase 1 of the expansion of debt, which starts from the production peak, essentially feeds on the valuation of real assets, since it coincides with the last phase of inflation acceleration: debt is incurred to buy buildings, gold, metals, forest products and oil, or to develop natural resources (as in Latin America, Africa, Indonesia).
- Phase 2 of the debt binge, which starts after prices have reached their peak and coincides with the feel-good era, feeds primarily on the increase in the value of financial assets caused by the first signs of disinflation: debt is used to play the stock market, to take over a company, or to pay loan interest.

These two sequences of debt expansion happen to coincide with the two halves of the production plateau, which can be best described as follows:

- The first half is bounded on the west by the production peak and on the east by the peak in prices.
- The second is bounded on the west by the price peak and on the east by the debt peak.

---

[27] Fisher, I.: 'The debt deflation theory of great depressions', Econometrica, vol 1, Paris (1933).

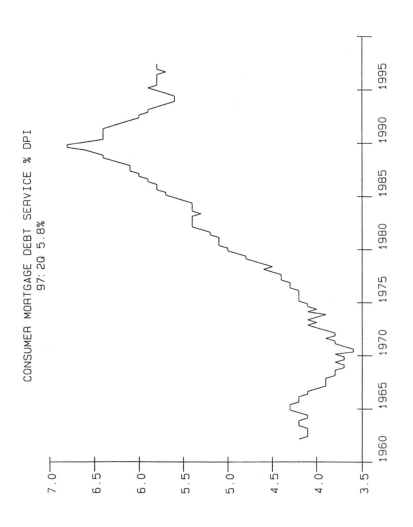

Figure 13. *Mortgage debt servicing of US households in percentage of disposable income from 1965 to 1997*

Source: International Strategy & Investment

In fact, what we suggest here is that debt growth follows a bell-shaped pattern of the same type and length as prices and production, but with an additional time lag.

Figure 13 is a perfect illustration of the long-term profile of total US debt growth from 1960 to 1996, and of the 'toppy' configuration that debt momentum had reached around 1990 in the United States. At the time, the same phenomenon was observed in Japan and the rest of the industrialized world.

It is then that we started to understand that the debt of the Third World (ie. approximately US$1500 billion) was small compared to that of the 'domestic Third World', which developed within the rich countries, and especially in Japan, where the next 'once in a century' crisis was brooding.

Coincidence of the debt peak and of a major stock market crash

Leverage is one of the prime engines of the financial bubble that characterizes the feel-good era and the second half of the plateau; as soon as it reaches maximum momentum, the engine chokes off for lack of fuel and the bubble explodes.

The peak of debt thus coincides, by its very nature, with a major stock exchange crash, whose impact on the real economy is devastating, since it is the beginning of the depression or 'creative destruction' phase. This mechanism of 'debt deflation', which one owes to Fisher, is described below, together with a chronological description of the third cycle.

We now have our 'marvellous clock', whose hands are supposed to indicate in sequential order the relative position of long-term prices, production and debt. We know that these hands move in an orderly fashion, according to an almost immutable choreography. Can this clock be useful to us? Can it really give us the 'economic time'?

It should be confronted with facts, past and present, without concessions.

3

The Test of History and the Pressure of the Current State of Affairs

A model is of no use unless it can stand the test of time and facts. In the case of the long cycle, two types of test have enabled us to confirm our convictions: confrontation with historical data on the one hand and with the current state of affairs on the other.

To be frank, if the lag that we underlined between prices and quantities is implicit in the thesis of Imbert, or if it receives the theoretical support of certain current disciples of Kondratieff, the confusion we depict above between prices and production is unfortunately not the prerogative of the man on the street. Even among some specialists, depression and deflation are often mixed up. Until very recently, and before Lutfalla co-authored his excellent work on the great stagnation of the 19th century,[28] the period 1873 to 1896 was referred to as the 'Great Depression', whereas this label applies really only to the decade 1873 to 1883, and not to the ensuing years (1883 to 1896), which is itself rather similar to the period 1837 to 1847. The latter was indeed characterized by a continuous fall in the general price level, but corresponding with resumption in growth, ie. in the production cycle: witness the railway mania of the early 1840s in London.

The paradox is only apparent. Japan of the mid-1980s is there to show us that healthy growth is not inconsistent with price deflation. Closer to us, the United States of the late 1990s gives us the same example of a 'deflationary boom'. This reinforces our vision of a structural de-phasing between growth and inflation. This de-phasing between two oscillatory

---

[28] Lutfalla, M.: 'La grande stagnation du XIXième siècle', Economica, Paris (1997).

parameters remains true, even if both can in practice enjoy long respites of synchronous fluctuations.

We can clarify the logic of our demonstration in three stages:

- On the basis of a chronological vision of the three preceding cycles, we show how each of them perfectly conforms to the pattern and successive phases of our model.
- We then proceed to a 'cross-sectional' analysis of these cycles by broad topic or phase type (stagflation, feel-good era, stock market crash, depression and golden age). We are helped in that by the heritage of popular imagery, whose scouring concision reflects from age to age the same stereotypes through the day's eyeglasses. Thus the Continental Blockade of 1807 to 1814 can be viewed as a primitive form of stagflation, similar to the period 1973 to 1980.
- With the test of history appearing conclusive, we then move to the most urgent topical question: are we presently living through the last moments (unpleasant besides) of the fourth Kondratieff?

The second section of this work is devoted to this essential question. We underline there a systematic parallel between the third and fourth cycles at 60-year intervals.

The chronology of the three preceding cycles

Now we move to review the cycles that we could trace back. The result of our research can be summarized in Figure 14.

Some definitions:
reflation: the period that follows a phase of deflation, therefore an absolute drop in prices, and which is marked by an easy monetary policy, low interest rates, liquidity injection in the banking system and currency depreciation.
depression: the period of contraction, or stagnation, of business activity, much longer and deeper than an ordinary business cycle recession, resulting from the dynamics of debt and asset deflation, usually at the end of a debt-driven financial bubble.

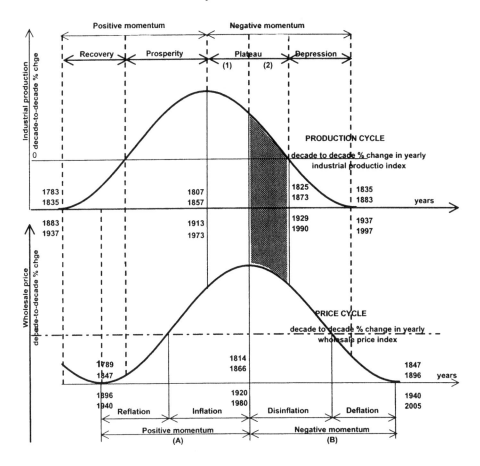

Figure 14. *Lags between prices and production from 1783 to date*

First cycle: 1783 to 1837

The depression in the early 1780s was due to the end of the overheating that arose from the US War of Independence (1776–81) and in particular from the blockade imposed by England on products from the fledgling republic of the United States. According to Kondratieff, price deflation lasted until 1789. However, the production cycle began its upturn in 1783. The period 1783 to 1789 was thus both the end of the price decline cycle and the beginning of the upturn in the volume cycle. The new growth momentum was supported by the first industrial applications of the steam engine, the mechanization of mills and the opening of new navigable waterways. England was then the prime mover of the Kondratieff wave.

The Napoleonic wars and the ensuing growth in economic activity and maritime trade (the golden age of the privateer) brought business momentum to its peak around 1807. Deceleration of growth began, accompanied by a resurgence of inflationary pressures, which reached their height in 1814 under the influence of the Continental Blockade (1807 to 1814) and the intensification of Anglo-French hostilities: this forms the inflationary part of the plateau. The price down wave[29] began in 1815, coinciding with the beginning of the second half of the plateau: after an initial recession (1817 to 1818) the feel-good era began, benefiting both from the final bursts of volume growth and from the first effects of disinflation. This was an ideal time for financial speculation due to a general downward trend in interest rates. This phase ended in 1825 with a stock market crash[30] originating in England following speculation in Latin America (yes, even in those days!). The collapse of raw materials (wheat and cotton in particular) and real estate triggered a depression that would last until 1837 for production and 1847 for prices. Furthermore, the rise of protectionism in France in 1822 increased the severity of the depression.

Second cycle: 1837 to 1883

Whereas the speculative and stock market excesses typical of a feel-good era marked the transition towards the next depression, the recovery of 1837 to 1847 was due to the effects of the Second Industrial Revolution. The simultaneous development of the railways, of coal mining and of the iron and steel industry firmly established England as the foremost industrial power. The opening of trading posts in Singapore (1819) and Hong Kong (1840) completed a worldwide network of warehouses and ports of call, whose main anchorage points were India to the east and Canada to the west – the two former jewels of the first French Colonial Empire, abandoned by Louis XV.

---

[29] Lutfalla, M.: 'Sommes-nous en 1815?', Revue d'Economie Politique, no.2 (1983).

[30] For the London crash of 1825, see Wolff, J.: 'Histoire économique de l'Europe', Economica, pp.368–369, Paris

England was not only the foremost industrial power, but also the leading trading partner. With the coronation of Queen Victoria in 1838, English dynamism imposed itself on the rest of the world, which then followed in its wake. It found an echo in particular in Guizot's[31] royal-bourgeois France ('Enrichissez-vous' or 'work, save and get rich'), not to mention the preferential relations that were then being re-established with the United States. It should not be forgotten that the industrial revival of the early 1840s was accompanied by continuing price deflation until at least 1843 and perhaps even 1849, if Kondratieff is to be believed. Taking the average of these two extremes, we can position the price trough in 1847, which coincides with the first gold discoveries in California. Industrial expansion continued under Napoleon III thanks to the Anglo-French free trade treaty. It fashioned a new economic landscape with its coal, steel and textile factories and its new infra-structures: railways, metal bridges, navigable waterways, ports and steamship lines. It fuelled land and real estate speculation and fostered a remodelling of the urban fabric (Haussmann in Paris). It gave birth to the large modern banking networks that are still around today (Comptoir d'Escompte, Société Générale in France) and specialized financial institutions (Crédit Foncier de France).

This expansion, at least in terms of momentum, reached a peak around 1857, ie. shortly after the Crimean War and during the Indian Mutiny. However, the peak of the price cycle did not occur until a few years later in 1865, shortly after the Mexican expedition (1864) and indeed the American Civil War.

The first half of the plateau phase, extending from 1857 to 1865, is marked by fairly sizeable financial and economic upheavals. The feel-good era began in 1866. It had to be a prosperous one in order for France to so quickly pay the five billion gold francs war penalty claimed by Germany in 1871. The depression of 1873 began with the bankruptcy of Creditanstalt of Vienna and lasted until 1883, at least as far as volumes were concerned.

---

[31] Prime Minister to French 'bourgeois' King Louis-Philippe around 1840.

Third cycle: 1883 to 1937

Just as the Second Industrial Revolution enjoyed a new boom (1837 to 1847) during the final price deflation stage of the preceding cycle, so the beginning of the third industrial cycle (1883 to 1896) coincided with the final price down wave of the second cycle that lasted until 1896. Thus, dawning economic growth benefited from the continuing low level of raw material prices and interest rates. It was the third 'deflationary boom' of its kind ever recorded since the Industrial Revolution.

The emergence of the automobile industry, the beginnings of aviation and electricity, in addition to the growth of the oil, chemical, iron and steel industries spearheaded the industrial renewal at the end of the century. The colonial rivalries in Africa and the Near East, which mirrored industrial competition, caused growth to accelerate. Victorian England was at the height of its power but France was vying for supremacy in Africa and the Mediterranean.

While Austria-Hungary was wobbling on its shaky foundations, the German Empire was consolidating its hold over central Europe and constructing a formidable naval fleet.

Basing its power on the coal of the Ruhr, Germany gradually caught up with England. The United States, licking its wounds from the Civil War, was in turn preparing for its stupendous rise in the 20th century.

The trough in the price cycle in 1896 coincided with monumental gold discoveries in South Africa, which enabled England to justify a long and costly war of attrition against the Boers in order to gain control.

In 1913, at the eve of the cataclysm that was to change the face of the earth, the industrial cycle was at its peak. Under the influence of World War I, inflation accelerated tremendously, peaking in 1920.

As already discussed, the 1920 to 1929 period was typical of a feel-good era, such as 1815 to 1825 or 1866 to 1873, which were marked by disinflation and an illusory feeling of well-being.

These three periods, which proved an ideal time for financial and stock market speculation, all led to a depression. The 1929 Wall Street crash is still considered the archetypal end to such periods of transition, the October 1987 'accident' being unable to remove it from the spotlight.

Only the Tokyo crash of 1990, by triggering the crisis of the 1990s, can be viewed as both the real echo and rival to Wall Street 1929.

We will leave the task of describing the course of the depression of the 1930s to Irving Fisher.[32] He describes the pattern of debt deflation as: 'distress' sales by private individuals; a portion of the proceeds is used to repay part of their bank indebtedness; this is followed by a decrease in bank deposits, ie. an element of the money supply; a decrease in the general price level also results; causing a decline in the net worth of businesses and hence bankruptcies; this also leads to a drop in profits, which often become losses; production, sales and employment will then decrease, thus destroying confidence a little more; once again slowing down the circulation of the reduced money supply. Fisher concludes that this will give rise to 'complicated movements' in interest rates: if nominal rates drop, real rates rise.

Thus, our chronological description of the first three cycles ends here. Before asking whether there is such a thing as a fourth Kondratieff, whose greatest merit would be to help us fare better in our own lives, we need to view the historical data all over again, but from a different perspective. This time, we will leave chronology aside for a while and concentrate on a cross-sectional or thematic approach.

A cross-sectional or thematic approach to the long waves

With the regularity of a clock, a few major economic themes come to the fore every 50 to 60 years. The mood of the day, fashion, or some particular circumstance, can alter them slightly, but the essence of the signal remains the same.

We have delineated five topics of this type, which popular wisdom or history books have embedded in our collective memories. You know these topics already, for they underlie the logic of our model. History has kept a record of them, in her own way, as the following tableaus

---

[32] Quoted in Lutfalla, M.: 'Sommes-nous à la veille d'une grande déflation?', SEDEIS (July 1985)

demonstrate. What is striking here, however, is the emerging shadow, in dotted lines so to speak, of an as yet unvalidated fourth Kondratieff, at least for its down wave.

With each theme, we associate four illustrations, one for each cycle.

Theme 1: The 30-year production up wave

1945 to 1973: the post-war miracle years
1885 to 1913: la Belle Epoque (goldilocks economy)
1837 to 1860: Victorian Fête
1783 to 1807: the first Industrial Revolution

Long expansion up wave, carried by an underlying technological revolution and a demographic rejuvenation: it is punctuated by the fluctuations of the business cycle.

If we must illustrate this theme, we would choose the recurring exploits here, at 50- to 60-year intervals, of the bee-type 'generations', who work, save and invest, shaping up the economic landscape for the next cycle.

1783: the exploits of the Montgolfier brothers (first balloon flight)
1860: the legend of Cutty Sark-type Clippers
1909: first airborne flight across the English Channel by Blériot
1954: a Toyota assembly-plant in the Tokyo area

Theme 2: The 'stagflation' era (seven years): growth slowdown and hyperinflation.

1973 to 1980: Oil shock
1913 to 1920: World War I
1857 to 1865: Top of cycle type conflicts
1807 to 1814: Continental Blockade

Brutal but structural growth deceleration due to an external shock of world proportions, creating a dynamics of scarcity while igniting military confrontations and inflationary expectations, the latter eventually rolling over after reaching a climax.

Most illustrations of this theme have a common leitmotiv: the blockade concept, which one repeatedly comes across at the top of each Kondratieff production cycle.

A good example of this type of environment was the Continental Blockade of 1807 to 1814, whereby Napoleon tried to cut England off from 'Euroland' supplies, triggering higher prices and slower growth. As a fine anecdotal episode of that period, we call to mind the seizure in the Gulf of Bengal of *HMS Kent*, a 37-gun vessel manned by 437 English regulars, by the legendary Surcouf on his 18-gun, 130-manned privateer *La Confiance*, from Saint-Malo.

Another famous naval blockade was imposed by the United States on their Confederate foes during the War of Secession, leading among others to the shipwreck of *SS Alabama* at the conclusion of a naval action off the French coast at Cherbourg in 1865.

During World War I, allied merchant ships were under heavy pressure from German U-boat attacks, in what amounted to a serious blockade. In that framework, we have singled out the heroic resistance of merchant ship *Kleber,* a three-mast schooner, which, after incurring heavy losses, managed to sail back to port free, as reported by *L'Illustration* on 13 October 1917.

Finally, as you will recall, the stagflation era of the 1970s started with the OPEC-imposed oil embargo, which was decided in the aftermath of the Yom Kippur War of 1973. Once again, a naval blockade of some sort!

Theme 3: The feel-good era and the speculative bubble: 7 to 10 years

1980 to 1989: the Japanese bubble
1920 to 1929: the US house of cards
1865 to 1873: the Austro-German bubble (led to 1873 Wiener crash)
1815 to 1825: post-Napoleonic feel-good breather

The beginning of price disinflation and the ensuing fall in interest rates triggers a psychological relief and a rise in financial assets, which fuels some kind of false prosperity, notwithstanding a still disappointing real world. Then the rising tide of debt leads the real estate and financial bubble to a climax. As soon as leverage reaches a maximum, the bubble bursts, the market crashes. Since the 1780s we have earmarked only four stock market crashes of world magnitude of this type: London (1825), Vienna (1873), Wall Street (1929) and Tokyo (1990).

Collective memory landmarks of the bubble type:

- The Japanese bubble: the 1990 purchase of a US$75 million Van Gogh.
- The 1920s US house of cards: the investment trust speculative pyramid.
- Pan-European bubble: the fragility of the financial empire of the Péreire brothers in 1867 as a harbinger of things to come.
- The post-Napoleonic breather: Latin-American mining speculations in London.

Theme 4: The depression or 'creative destruction phase': 7 to 10 years

1990 to 1997: Japanese depression
1930 to 1937: The 1930s
1873 to 1883: Great Depression of the 19th Century
1825 to 1835: Dickensian squalor

The crash pulls the real economy into recession by initially rocking the banking system, sick of debt deflation. De-leveraging is the key word of this depression phase, marked by waves of bankruptcies and lay-offs and by the exacerbation of competition. The drop in prices hurts margins. Beyond the social fracture that these upheavals produce, the leavens of the following structural rebound are sewn, through a change in mentalities and the openings of technical change.

Usually, this period tends to heighten the feud between socialism and liberalism.

Public excuses of Yamaichi President in December 1997
The Grapes of Wrath by Steinbeck
Birth of trade unionism (passing of Trade Union Act, 1871)
David Copperfield by Dickens

Theme 5: Golden age or deflationary boom: promise or reality?

1997 to 2003?
1945 to 1956
1885 to 1896
1837 to 1848

The lag that we observe between the long production cycle and the price wave allows at the end of the preceding phase an ideal configuration where structural growth rebounds as disinflation continues: thus, the 'golden age'.

This privileged period is the first stage of a new 30-year phase of prosperity.

Microsoft prosperity: Windows 97
The Eisenhower years: 1953 to 1960
The Berlin Colonial Conference: 1884
The railway mania: 1840 to 1845

Is there such thing as a fourth Kondratieff cycle: 1937 to 1997?

Once again, we touch here at the heart of the raison d'être of this book, which is to suggest the possibility of a radical change in economic conditions, for the better this time.

It is necessary to try and explain the rationale of the current situation, because it generates despair at the worst possible moment since, according to our belief, the worst of the crisis is behind us. Mrs Forrester,[33] why didn't you write your book in 1989, when the climactic phase of the down wave started in 1973 was brooding? Then, it would have been useful to prepare us for what awaited us. Today, your book is only the mirror in which you reflect to society its instantaneous image: a mirror? I should say a rear-view mirror.

To tell the truth, the success of your book, of which, beyond your art of writing, I admire the scouring descriptive power, is for me the visible

---

[33] Forrester, V.: 'L'horreur économique', Fayard, Paris (1996).

sign of a 'fait accompli', in the sense that stockbrokers use to mean that an event is already discounted. If your idea received such welcome applause, it must be because it flatters the air of time, the ambient feeling. Isn't it a modern echo of the great Malthusian fears, and of the 19th-century rearguard fight of the Lyons silk workers for whom technical progress was already synonymous with unemployment? On the contrary, we believe that progress will create more and more sophisticated jobs and that the real democratization of knowledge will mean the ensuing democratization of creativity, and hence the ennoblement of work – of all types of work; and by no means 'the End of Work'.[34]

This is why we realize that the time has come for us to put on our rose-tinted glasses for the first time since 1973 and view the world differently. Let us look at what is occurring in the United States, Britain, Canada and Mexico – not to mention the rest of Latin America, and even Asia, where a painful auditing of accounts has started. Europe is not the centre of the world any more; the rest of the world is taking off using good old liberal recipes, and the time has come for continental Europe to benefit too, not to mention a desperately lagging Japan.

We are all the more confident in our message of hope today as we were eager to underline in 1989 the risks that the industrial world was running because of its debt overhang.

We are only following some type of 'Ariane's rope' along the down wave in the labyrinth of economic fluctuations. The excellent parallel that we noted between our model and historical data, was the first step in the process of proving the existence of a formal determinism leading irresistibly to a return of structural prosperity in the near future.

From our model of the relationship between production, prices and debt, we have extracted four central concepts, aside from that of a 30-year up wave, and which illustrate the different stages of the down wave:

- Stagflation, where growth deceleration and hyperinflation coexist.
- Feel-good era leading to a financial bubble.
- A stock market crash of world proportions, as a direct outgrowth of the preceding bubble.
- Depression or creative destruction phase.

[34] Rifkin, John, *The End of Work*, Putnam Publishing (1995).

From now on, we will view these concepts with their chained sequential order as necessary constituents of our Ariane's rope in qualifying any possible down wave. Thus, the second step of our demonstration will be articulated around the following points:

• Taking for granted that the 30 'miracle years' from 1945 to 1973 are the ascending wave of a fourth Kondratieff cycle, we show that the long crisis that started in 1973 is fully qualified as typical of an almost complete down wave of the latest cycle.
• It must then follow that the whole period 1937 to 1997 can be regarded as representative of a fourth complete Kondratieff cycle.
• If such is the case, the current depression phase is nothing but the prelude of the next up wave, ie. of the ascending phase of the fifth cycle.

It will have been understood that the Achilles heel of our demonstration lies in the first point, for once this link is connected, the rest must follow.

Why the 1973 to 1997 period qualifies as the down wave of the latest cycle

The course of the long crisis begun in 1973 awakens in us a powerful feeling of déjà vu in its major phases and turning points. This in turn leads us to make four parallels, showing how faithfully, at 60-year intervals, history seems to repeat itself:

• First parallel, between the 1910s and the 1970s: what are the similarities, from an economic point of view, between the shock of World War I and the oil shock of 1973? Answer: an inflationary slowdown, the advent of a dynamics of scarcity, a great wasting of resources, the exasperation of antagonisms, and a worldwide 'new deal'.
• Second parallel, between the 1920s and the 1980s, or the illustration of the concept of a feel-good era or speculative prosperity. We will concentrate on this point at length.

- Third parallel: Wall Street 1929 and Tokyo 1990.
- Final parallel, between the 1930s and the 1990s, or the illustration of the concept of depression, such as the one Japan still lives through today, or until recently, that of continental Europe.

These comparisons make up our second section, entitled 'The Magnificent Parallels', each one being dedicated to a separate chapter.

Part Two

The Magnificent Parallels Between The Third And Fourth Cycles And Why Our Depression Is Waning

The Magnificent Parallels Between the Third and Fourth Cycles and Why Our Depression is Waning

To sum up, it is generally agreed that the depression of the third cycle lasted until 1937, and that the industrial cycle took again its ascending phase at the eve of World War II. Between 1937 and 1940, the price cycle continued its descent. The ascending phase of the industrial cycle lasted from 1937 to 1973, despite the interruption of war. From 1945 to 1973, the industrialized countries enjoyed some 30 years of prosperity, certainly intersected with recessions of the business cycle, but without any questioning of the basic up trend, nor of the way the 'pie' was being shared. These are our 30 'miracle years', remote echo of 'la Belle Epoque' of 1885 to 1913, or of the 'Victorian fête' of 1837 to 1860. The end of this period was marked by a most decisive event: the oil crisis of 1973, which symbolized the questioning of the way the pie was being shared, at least among countries, and blocked the growth process. This was the beginning of a long down wave, which we are still in today, but that one can break down into three successive phases intersected with two major turning points: 1980 and 1990.

- From 1973 to 1980, the crisis starts with two symmetrical moves: a growth slowdown and a violent acceleration of inflation, in what amounts to a malefic criss-cross. It is the inflationary phase of the plateau. One could baptize it the 'rust age', as opposed to the golden age, which, at the end of the crisis, is marked by the opposite criss-cross. But its current name is the 'era of stagflation'. It is the purpose of a first parallel between the Great War years and the 1970s. 1980 is a major turning point, since it marks the peak of inflation and the beginning of the second phase of the plateau. There too, a comparison is essential with the year 1920, inflation top of the third cycle.

- From 1980 to 1990 extends the disinflation phase of the plateau, or the feel-good era. The fall in interest rates, generated by disinflation, causes an irrepressible tide of debt, which fuels both real estate and stock exchange speculation, especially in Tokyo this time, and creates the mirage of a transitory prosperity, on paper. This prosperity mirage is in sharp contrast to the continued deterioration of the real economy. Hence, the birth of a financial bubble, an ideal terrain for the next major stock market crash, whose advanced notice will be given, in this case, by the October 1987 warning. 1990 marks an end to the feel-good era, triggered by the Tokyo crash and a debt peak. It is the start of an asset deflation spiral that will push Japan into a depression, out of which it has yet to emerge. The similarity to Wall Street 1929 is amazing.

- From 1990 on extends the 'creative destruction' phase, marked by strong deflationary and recessionary pressures. These last are not only due to the unwinding of the debt excess of the 1980s, but also to the overkill attempts by some central banks still eager to fight the last war. This period, which was still going on as late as October 1998, has great similarities with the 1930s, even if the deflationary shock is currently more unequally distributed than at the time. Russia, Japan and continental Europe, in that order, were the most affected countries, together with emerged Asia. The Anglo-American countries have remained relatively unaffected by the crisis. The comparison between the 1990s and the 1930s will undoubtedly prove one day to be a great classic.

4

A Parallel Between the 1910s and the 1970s: Stagflation Time

The revolt of the oil producers in 1973 made sense: their purpose was to tell the industrialized countries that there was a price to pay for the abandonment of the monetary discipline of Bretton Woods, and in particular of the gold convertibility of the US dollar on 15 August 1971. The price was this 'rusty cross', which was to symbolize the 1970s, with growth deceleration on the one hand and subsequent rising inflation on the other. This malefic chiasma was going to inaugurate a long lasting down wave for Western economies, which to some extent they are still in today. Ever since, the spectrum of inflation has not ceased haunting our economies and our finance ministers, even if the problem appears largely behind us today. Unfortunately, inflation had itself generated another plague in its trail: over-indebtedness, resulting from the abandonment of budgetary disciplines at all levels – government, household and corporation.

Inflation and debt are thus the two fundamental factors of the demise of real growth, acting successively like the two blades of an avenging sickle. This is why the production deceleration phase throughout the industrial plateau is carried out in two phases, which, for different and sometimes opposed reasons, call into question the current wealth and revenue sharing scheme.

In the first half of the plateau, or stagflation era, the economic slowdown triggers, or accompanies, a dynamics of scarcity that leads to the exasperation of selfishness and to the aggravation of antagonisms.

At an international level, we observe the advent of cleavages between countries:

- Monetary cleavages in the 1970s, between hard currency and soft currency countries, symbolized by the rise of Japan.
- Military cleavages in the 1910s, in the wake of political alliances or of battles lost or won, coinciding with the emergence of the United States as a world power from 1918 onwards.

At an economic level, one observes a downward shift in the supply schedule, either because of an explosion of unemployment (in the 1970s), or of the massive conscription enrolments of World War I.

At a financial level, one notes the persistent distress of the equity and bond markets, and a rush for real assets whose price appreciation benefits from debt-fed speculation.

In the second half of the plateau, this upheaval causes a political backlash that calls for the demise of the dynamics of scarcity, the advent of disinflation and the implementation of supply-side policies.[35]

On the eve of the oil crisis the industrialized countries were euphoric. It was the era of the European miracle, whether it be German-made, or Italian, not to mention the fantastic growth extrapolations by Data Resources for France. Japan, on the other hand, had started to take off for real, but still without disputing US supremacy. It was Galbraith[36] who described the 'affluent society' of the 1960s being extended to an inner circle of privileged countries, where unemployment was non-existent. Economic prosperity was such that the 'baby boomers' of the time could afford the luxury of yawning at the consumer society.

However, when the thunderclap of OPEC's oil embargo came to streak this too blue azure, the die had already been cast – indeed, this had been the case since the abandonment by Washington in 1971 of the monetary discipline of Bretton Woods. Sixty years earlier, World War I had got rid of another monetary discipline, although more than 100 years old in France and England: the gold standard.

---

[35] As a consequence, this would logically lead Ronald Reagan to implement supply-side policies in the 1980s, as a remote echo of similar policies by US Presidents Harding and Coolidge in the 1920s.

[36] Galbraith, J.K.: 'The Great Crash, 1929', The Riverside Press, Cambridge (1954)

The abandonment of monetary discipline and the explosion of inflation

One of the main purposes of a currency is its function as a store of value in order to guarantee equity between debtors and creditors, and to facilitate the transfers of value over time, which is the purpose of saving.

To erase the value of the currency is akin to tearing off the social contract. It is, however, the most widespread mistake of economic history. Kondratieff explains that the very existence of these long price cycles clearly testifies to the ancestral inclination of countries and governments to avoid refunding their debts by the systematic use of devaluation. Regularly thus, the social body seems to stubbornly indulge in repeating the same errors.

In fact, wars generally tend to exhaust public finances and inflate borrowing requirements, swelling public debt and, in practice, forcing recourse to devaluation. In the present case, the Vietnam War (1965–73), like World War I before it, had all the attributes of a top of cycle type war, acting as an inflation generator.

There is a clear relationship between inflation control and the problem of wealth and revenue distribution.

A price up wave favours debtors and handicaps creditors and rentiers.

The rising generations, who have no net financial assets as yet, benefit from rising inflation with the proviso of taking out loans at fixed rates.

On the contrary, declining generations, as holders of the bulk of net financial assets, usually benefit from disinflation, and otherwise can defend their purchasing power by lending at variable rates or taking refuge in real assets: gold, real estate, etc.

Thus the age wave side of the revenue distribution equation confirms our findings in Chapter 1 on the relationships between the life cycle and long wave theory.

Did the inflation up wave that accompanied World War I and which culminated in 1920 have demographic causes? At the time, Germany, whose population was young and growing, was already vocal about the need for 'vital space', a theme that would continue through the 1930s. This price wave, exacerbated by the globalization of conflict, would end up putting an end to a monetary system, the gold standard, which had withered across a whole century, from 1803 to 1914.

The Korean War-related wavelet of 1951 was readily absorbed thanks to the monetary discipline of the newly created Bretton Woods agreements. On the other hand, the subsequent abandonment of this system at the beginning of the 1970s led to a true beachcomber which culminated in 1980, and which took 18 years to get under control – only partially. Could this abandonment have been avoided? We believe not, for reasons that are due to the regularity of the Kondratieff cycles, and to the kind of invisible hand that controls the primary trends of the economy. In some ways, Kondratieff's clock is relentless: both for the worst and for the best. In 1973 it was for the worst.

The sudden rise in oil prices – a tripling in a few months – had the effect on Western economies of an unforeseen tax rise, of a toll on the purchasing power of economic agents, with immediate recessive consequences. However, to soften the effects of this shock for the populations, economic authorities then generally decided to loosen a notch on their already accommodating monetary and budgetary policies. This would lead to the irresistible acceleration of price rises in all OECD countries, and to a new oil crisis in the period 1979 to 1980, the whole episode in a slowdown context compared to the previous miracle decades: in brief, what it led to was 'stagflation' in all its splendour.

By the same token, World War I, not to mention its appalling casualties and subsequent demographic long-term impact, hit the belligerents as a three-fold economic shock: first, the collapse of the civilian labour force, then a much lower national income as a result, and finally a negative wealth effect through the fall of financial assets.

The rise of antagonisms and the race for real assets

Logically, the contraction of the pie to be shared led to an exasperation of antagonisms, equally on international as on social or financial stages. Once again, Kondratieff's clock was ticking, watching for the spectre of protectionism, unemployment, of war even, to loom for real. We saw earlier how cycle peaks had consistently favoured the outbreak of war. The logic is as follows: at the top of the cycle, accumulated capital is a maximum and financial wealth reaches a peak. Hence, capitalizing on their financial power, states or governments are enticed into territorial expansion strategies. In addition, the contraction of trade outlets, due to the developing stagflation, irritates their aggressiveness. This was especially true in 1914. Fortunately, 60 years later, the field of competition moved away from military into another type of conflict: a certainly pitiless, but velvet-gloved economic war.

The word 'stagflation' correctly translates this 'rust age', in which one loses on all grounds: on growth and inflation, of course, but also in terms of traditional financial assets.

Increased international competition

The oil tax imposed on rich countries did not cause concerted reaction from them, such as would for example the creation of a cartel of purchasers. Not only did the Western countries face OPEC in dispersed order, each one trying to play its own cards, but they also embarked on a wild commercial war, each vying for control of the newly rich outlets of the Near East and of the world supply of advanced industrial products.

Very quickly, this crisis revealed a cleavage, within the rich countries, between trade surplus and deficit countries: on the one hand, Germany and Japan, on the other, France and Anglo-Saxon countries. This cleavage was exacerbated by growing US-Japan trade frictions, an economic counterpart of the politico-military duel between Russians and Americans. This double competition culminated at the end of the 1980s and ended clearly in both cases to the benefit of the United States. There is a perfect analogy between the Japan–US competition of the 1980s and the fight for supremacy in the 1920s between the United States and Britain. In fact, in both cases this parallel traced its source to ten years earlier: just as World War I had shaken the dominant role of Britain and supported the rise of America, so the oil crisis of 1973 initially challenged the supremacy of the United States and opened the way for Japan's ascent.

Japan–US competition, as a reflection of the more general cleavage outlined above, was born from the oil crisis and fed from the dynamics of scarcity observed until 1980; it largely survived the advent of disinflation and extended until the crash of Tokyo in 1990. Indeed, even if Japan had built its competitive advantage on the back of some US weaknesses – especially the negative budget impact of a gigantic US military build-up, from which itself was exempt – it nevertheless remained a fragile giant, as the Gulf crisis would reveal. The combined rise of the US dollar and oil, observed in the aftermath of the Gulf War, hit the heart of Japan's financial system and, through a spectacular crash, led it into a lengthy depression.

Flare up of social tensions

Just as World War I lay at the origin of upheavals of a radical nature, ringing the death knell in Europe of a civilization still largely rural and aristocratic,[37] so the oil crisis of 1973 was a source of considerable change. The inflationary push that went with it put large numbers of small and medium-sized firms out of business for not adjusting fast enough to the new challenges of this world. In turn, these bankruptcies triggered a tidal wave of unemployment, which still today has not really ebbed in Europe, a remote echo of European social disturbances shortly after the Treaty of Versailles[38] in 1919.

The race between prices and wages, by durably affecting the breakdown of added value within companies, ended in a durable weakening of the financial health of the latter. One had to wait for the psychological reversal of the 1980s to timidly start to regain lost ground in this field. Meanwhile, the macroeconomic counterpart of these social disturbances held in the sometimes uncontrolled increase in public expenditure and deficits. The phenomenon was universal at first.

The feel-good era of the 1980s contributed little to the reduction of unemployment, in Europe at least. As for the depression phase of the 1990s, it still worsened the 'social fracture' between the unemployed and others and uncovered new categories of poor, and this, in alarming numbers to date.

---

[37] cf. Jean Renoir's film *'La grande illusion'*.

[38] cf. the Weimar Republic in Germany, or the ascent of the 'Cartel des Gauches' in France in the early 1920s.

The distress of financial markets and the rush for real assets

Just as the war of 1914 had led to the collapse of the belligerents' national income and financial assets, similarly the oil crisis shook the financial markets over a decade, from 1973 to 1982. Indeed, as the dynamics of scarcity favours debtors at the expense of creditors, everyone understands that it takes only leverage to grow rich by accumulating real assets, which are used as protection against inflation: gold, real estate, land, natural resources, food etc. This rush for real assets, while prejudicial for the financial markets, thus really ignited the first phase of debt expansion from 1973 to 1980. During this period, financial markets experienced a negative performance, in bonds in particular. On the other hand, in eight years, from August 1971 to December 1980, the price of gold moved from US$35 to US$800 per ounce, witness to investors' growing craze for real assets.

After a lapse in time, however, this patrimonial logic, which handicapped both the middle class and the rentiers, while erasing their purchasing power, soon became politically intolerable. The climate was ripe for a reaction. By inaugurating the disinflation and feel-good era, Ronald Reagan symbolized this turning point in 1981, as Warren Harding had done before him in 1921.

What subsequently became of the other plague of our economies, second only to inflation, namely the debt overhang, and its counterpart, the abandonment of all budgetary disciplines? We will examine this in Chapter 5, wherein the dialectics of the financial bubble will be exposed at length.

5

Parallel Between the 1920s and the 1980s: Variations on the Theme of the Feel-Good Era Leading to a Financial Bubble

The peak of inflation, terminal end to the era of stagflation, is a major turning point for the long cycle, for it coincides with a powerful demographic reversal as the dominant age groups start to grey. Here we refer again to Chapter 1, Figure 8, demonstrating the excellent parallel between the age wave cycle and the price cycle in the United States. After having widely benefited from the inflation tide of previous decades, these greying populations gently adopt the rentier profile, and, from now on, demand policies of monetary stability. This is the way disinflation policies are enacted in the first place, leading to the 'competitive disinflation era', an expression which perfectly summarizes the two ingredients of the policy mix in vogue at this stage of the cycle: monetary tightening, on the one hand, but softened for the consumer by supply-side inspired tax cut policies,[39] on the other.

However, viewed from corporations, the fight for supply–side leadership on a world scale eventually ends up putting whole segments of non-competitive industries out of business: in short, the production down wave continues, even worsens, and the industrial world becomes pitiless. On the other hand, the financial 'sphere' is prosperous, due to the fall in rates, and because it is easier to make a fortune quickly and without

---

[39] Chevallier, F.-X.: 'Politique de l'offre au Japon', Revue d'Economie Politique (June 1982).

effort there, in particular due to the use of leverage. This is why this phase of the cycle is rich in contradictions: basically, the real crisis continues, but it is masked by a secondary, or fictitious, prosperity, which owes much to trading room 'golden boys and girls', and to real estate tycoons; hence, the expression 'bubble years'. However, as this prosperity is based on debt – the continuous fall in rates encouraging both borrowers and creditors – it creates a house of cards,[40] a financial bubble, from there on uncheckable. When leverage comes to saturation, the bubble bursts, the house of cards falls apart: it's crash time.

Parallel with the 1920s: Initiation

The crash of October 1987 sensitized us to the relevance of a parallel with the 1920s. The economist Ed Hyman, then vice-chairman of the brokerage firm Cyrus Lawrence, had taken the lead in this matter since 1985 by showing that at a 59-year interval, the Dow Jones index seemed to repeat its performances by a factor of ten. In addition, an extrapolation of his diagram suggested a possible crash in 1987 or 1988.

At the scale of the long wave, this precision was extraordinary, even if the crash of 1987 was not for good. For us, it was a warning and we knew we had entered a critical zone, one which Japanese events of 1990 were going to brilliantly confirm.

Figure 15 exposes a parallel between the highs and lows of the Dow Jones index from 1912 to 1930, on the left, and the same parameters for the period 1971 to 1989, on the right.

Until 1985, the date when the table was drawn, the two series were very similar, to a factor of ten. By extrapolating the series over the then unknown period 1986 to 1989, while multiplying by ten the data of the years 1927 to 1930, Hyman clearly hinted at a potential problem between 1987 and 1988.

The economist Ravi Batra, in his book entitled 'The great depression of the 1990s', written in 1986, also established a parallel between the two feel-good decades, which we reproduce in Figure 16.

---

[40] As creditors' assets keep inflating with the downturn trend in interest rates.

Year	Low	High	Year	Low	High	
1930	158	294	1989	1580	2940	
1929	199	381	1988	1990	3810	Interpolation
1928	191	300	1987	1910	3000	
1927	153	202	1986	1530	2020	
1926	135	167	1985	1185	1553	
1925	115	159	1984	1087	1287	
1924	88	121	1983	1027	1267	} Lift-off
1923	86	105	1982	777	1071	
1922	79	103	1981	824	1024	
1921	64	82	1980	759	1000	
1920	67	110	1979	797	898	
1919	79	130	1978	742	908	
1918	74	89	1977	801	1000	
1917	66	99	1976	859	1015	
1916	85	110	1975	632	882	
1915	54	99	1974	878	892	} Crunch
1914	71	83	1973	788	1052	
1913	72	89	1972	889	1036	
1912	80	94	1971	798	951	} Introduction

Figure 15. *An extraordinary parallel between the fluctuations of the Dow Jones index at 59-year intervals*

To better emphasize the parallels between the 1920s and 1980s, it may be useful to recall the anecdotal character of these similarities. In so doing, we underline the two essential ingredients which these mythical decades share in common and which fully qualify them as feel-good eras or bubble years: the combination of disinflation and over-indebtedness on the one hand, the rise and fall of the financial sphere on the other.

Anecdotal similarities

The first similarity with the 1920s is due to the political environment marked by the strong personality of Ronald Reagan, who embodied so well the universal free market revolution of the 1980s. Taking up his duties in January 1981, Reagan made no mystery of his ideological affinities with Presidents Harding and Coolidge, the two most symbolic

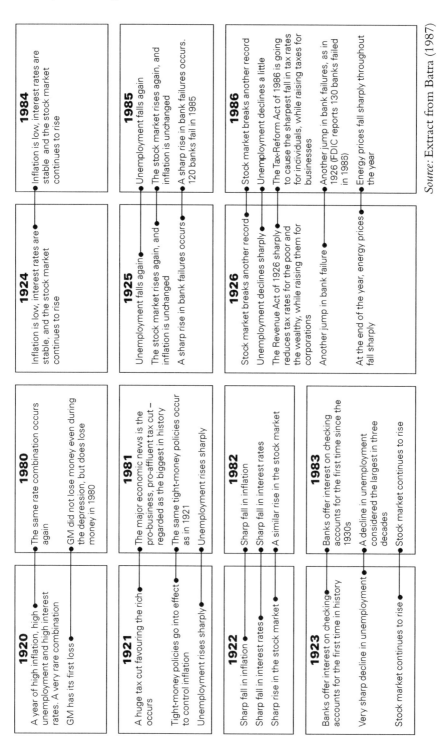

1920
- A year of high inflation, high unemployment and high interest rates. A very rare combination
- GM has its first loss

1980
- The same rate combination occurs again
- GM did not lose money even during the depression, but does lose money in 1980

1984
- Inflation is low, interest rates are stable and the stock market continues to rise

1921
- A huge tax cut favouring the rich occurs
- Tight-money policies go into effect to control inflation
- Unemployment rises sharply

1981
- The major economic news is the pro-business, pro-affluent tax cut – regarded as the biggest in history
- The same tight-money policies occur as in 1921
- Unemployment rises sharply

1985
- Unemployment falls again
- The stock market rises again, and inflation is unchanged
- A sharp rise in bank failures occurs. 120 banks fall in 1985

1924
- Inflation is low, interest rates are stable, and the stock market continues to rise

1925
- Unemployment falls again
- The stock market rises again, and inflation is unchanged
- A sharp rise in bank failures occurs

1922
- Sharp fall in inflation
- Sharp fall in interest rates
- Sharp rise in the stock market

1982
- Sharp fall in inflation
- Sharp fall in interest rates
- A similar rise in the stock market

1986
- Stock market breaks another record
- Unemployment declines a little
- The Tax-Reform Act of 1986 is going to cause the sharpest fall in tax rates for individuals, while raising taxes for businesses
- Another jump in bank failures, as in 1926 (FDIC reports 130 banks failed in 1985)
- Energy prices fall sharply throughout the year

1926
- Stock market breaks another record
- Unemployment declines sharply
- The Revenue Act of 1926 sharply reduces tax rates for the poor and the wealthy, while raising them for corporations
- Another jump in bank failure
- At the end of the year, energy prices fall sharply

1923
- Banks offer interest on checking accounts for the first time in history
- Very sharp decline in unemployment
- Stock market continues to rise

1983
- Banks offer interest on checking accounts for the first time since the 1930s
- A decline in unemployment considered the largest in three decades
- Stock market continues to rise

Source: Extract from Batra (1987)

Figure 16. *The 60-year cycle: The 1920s vs. the 1980s*

characters of the 'roaring 20s':[41] with their portraits firmly planted in the Oval Office. Is it pure chance if such twin policies were designed and implemented at the top of a long price up wave: the first, after the inflation high of 1920, the second, after prices peaked out in 1980? Incidentally, this parallel lends Kondratieff's long wave theory more relevance. Let us return to 1980. One of the President's most influential advisors, Arthur Laffer, father of the famous curve (showing that too much tax kills fiscal receipts) and emblematic promoter of 'supply-side' theories,[42] spent much of his time 'roadshowing' across the world to spread the good news and advocate these glowing references to the 1920s. Supply-side policies, tax reform, deregulation and monetary discipline (the 'price rule') were the basic pillars of the doctrine. In practice, all it took was Reagan's ability and daring to stay the course and implement this programme throughout his mandate, tearing off from Congress his decisive Tax Reform Act of 1986, which, in retrospect, can be viewed as somehow equivalent to the Tax Revenue Act of 1926.

The second similarity between the two periods is that both start at the top of the price up wave: 1920 for the first and 1980 for the second. They thus happen to coincide with the first signs of disinflation; for, in both cases, political leaders received a clear mandate from their constituents to get rid of inflation.

In addition, both periods begin with recessions of comparable magnitude: 1921 to 1922 for one, 1981 to 1982 for the other. Each of these recessions combines the extremely rare conjunction of a record rate of unemployment, together with a high rate of inflation, the sum of both adding to what is called the 'misery index'. In both cases, this misery indicator will fall, from one end to the other, from 20 per cent to less than 10 per cent. In both cases, this result is obtained by the conjunction of several measures: price liberalization, corporate deregulation, tax cuts and support for monetary discipline. In both cases, supply–side policies are at work.

---

[41] Roaring 20s: another image reflecting the 'bubble' prosperity of the 'feel-good era' and one which would also be used in the Reagan years six decades later (roaring 80s).

[42] Policies aimed at fostering production, labour and individual entrepreneurship, through fiscal incentives, as opposed to demand–led packages.

The parallel between Tokyo 1990 and Wall Street 1929 is the third paradoxical similarity with the 1920s. At the time, Britain was still the dominant power and the United States disputed her financial primacy. At the close of the 1980s it was Tokyo's turn to dispute Wall Street's supremacy. As at 31 March 1989 Tokyo's stock market capitalization was worth around US$3900 billion against US$2600 billion for New York, ie. 50 per cent more. On the same day, the Tokyo Stock Exchange weighed approximately half of the world market capitalization (approximately US$8000 billion). The relative weight of the Japanese Bourse versus the rest of the world was thus at the time equivalent to that of Wall Street in 1929. We will elaborate later on the chronology of the Japanese stock exchange crisis. This perspective should not allow us to forget that, from an economic point of view, the United States remained the dominant power by far, an essential criterion for the analysis of the long cycle.

The final similarity is of an industrial and commercial nature. We all learned at school that the crisis of 1929 was an overproduction crisis, ie. stemming from oversupply compared to demand. It seems that the supply-side policies that were implemented all across the world, following in the wake of the United States, contributed to fostering a crisis of this nature in the 1990s. Sector by sector competition was exacerbated, successively forcing the car, steel, oil and chemical industries to restructure and continuously adjust throughout the decade, not to mention the spheres of electronics (general public or professional) or telecoms. This is the reason why the rapid overview between the 1920s and the 1980s will further cause us to consider another parallel: this time between the 1930s and the 1990s.

Disinflation and the tide of debt

Let us recall the essence of our model: the slowdown that extends throughout the plateau phase of industrial decay usually unfolds into two stages – the stagflation and bubble years – both of which contribute, albeit for different and sometimes contradictory reasons, to the upsetting of the revenue-sharing dynamics between labour and capital and also between nations. In the first half of the plateau, this slowdown creates a dynamics of scarcity leading to a flight for real assets, which exacerbates both individual frustrations and collective imbalances. In the second half of the plateau, the political backlash that these imbalances create calls for an end to this dynamic and for the implementation of the disinflation process, however painful it might be initially.

The latter implies a structural downtrend in interest rates, which, in turn, triggers two powerful moves reinforcing one another: an irresistible rise of the financial markets and an irrepressible appetite for debt. This is the stuff of which bubbles are made. The combination of these two factors leads successively to the rise and fall of the financial sphere[43] and, in the final analysis, to a new frailty of the markets, which in turn leads to a crash.

Insofar as inflation leads to increases in the face value of assets, it is a powerful incentive to take on debt, at the individual, corporate and government levels. It was quite natural, therefore, that the inflationary tidal wave of the 1970s carried with it the beginnings of a surge in debt. But it took the advent of disinflation in the 1980s for this surge to reach its full momentum.

The first manifestation of this phenomenon in the 1970s was the creation and rapid development of an uncontrolled mass of eurodollars, the currency favoured by industrial and financial multinationals, and whose misdeeds have often been denounced.[44]

As prime beneficiaries of the recycling of the eurodollars, then petrodollars, US banks vied with one another to service the riskier but, they hoped, more promising markets of the developing countries, in particular Latin America and Africa. However, the price of these countries' exportable commodities (agricultural products, energy, metals) followed the general downtrend of wholesale prices since 1980, and in fact declined considerably. Thus, well before the Japanese slid into depression, these countries had given us a valuable insight into the nature of a depression, with the combination of a dramatic fall in asset prices and a growing burden of debt.

---

[43] Let us refer again to Kondratieff's analysis of the French rente, especially between 1815 and 1830, or alternatively between 1873 and 1896, two periods which were characterized by an inflation and interest rate structural down wave, and hence by a structural up wave in the rente price.

[44] See Beckerman, G.: 'Les eurodollars', P.U.F., Paris (1992).

One would have been wrong to believe that the developed world would remain immune to these problems. The collapse of the Japanese banking system in the 1990s provides perfect proof to the contrary. This is because the industrial world had itself indulged in the fun of leveraging, starting from the mid-1980s.

At the beginning of a long price downtrend (ie. from 1981 or 1921), it is not real assets that are the craze anymore, but financial assets instead: equities and bonds. However, by construction, speculation is much better armed in the case of financial assets, which can be bought on margin, than for real assets. It is thus not surprising that debt growth was exponential, equally in the 1920s as in the 1980s. The ten-fold increase in Japanese banks' assets from 1980 to 1989 bears witness to this. By the same token, the commercial aggressiveness of US S&L institutions during the same period could be viewed as similar in nature, with, in both cases, a potential systemic crisis looming.

Thus, at the end of the 1980s, the crisis brewing in the industrialized world banking system revealed that Third World debt was small when

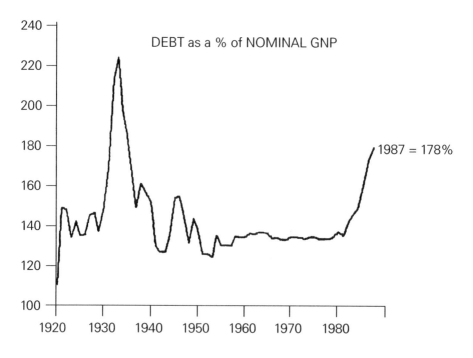

Figure 17. *US total debt as a percentage of GDP*

compared with the domestic debt excess of some industrialized countries, at least if one added national and private debt.

On this occasion, the existence of true 'internal Third Worlds' came to conspicuous light in particular with reference to the massive bad loan overhang of some US savings banks, not to mention most Japanese financial institutions. The banking bankruptcies of the 1930s immediately came to mind. In the case of the United States, for instance, the tide of debt was overwhelming and we recognized there the 'invisible hand' controlling Kondratieff's clock. If only the extent of the twin deficits had been less than household saving alone was able to accommodate, we would have seen it as a lesser evil. Unfortunately, US households chose to imitate the government, and the abandonment of budgetary discipline had become a cultural phenomenon, increasing the foreign trade deficit and inflating debt at individual, corporate and government levels.

Not since the 1930s had the total debt of the United States (relative to gross domestic product (GDP)) been as high as on the eve of the Gulf crisis. Government, corporate and household debt then totalled more than US$9000 billion, or approximately twice GDP, as shown in Figure 17, drawn from a study by Cyrus Lawrence in the late 1980s.

Once again, the clock was ticking along Kondratieff's lines.

Rise and fall of the financial sphere

The advent of the feel-good era in 1982 coincided with the promotion of what was called the 'financial sphere'. Exactly what was meant by this expression? Firstly, a concrete reality: the explosion of the financial markets, precipitated by a dramatic fall in interest rates from 1981 to 1986. Secondly, a new business philosophy ensuring the primacy of the financier on the industrialist, and opening the way towards a large restructuring effort from the largest industrial groups.

According to this philosophy, shareholder value becomes the paramount objective. Large investment banks benefit immensely from this trend that allows them to capitalize on their financial engineering expertise. It is not rare in this context to see the same company bought and resold several times in a short time span, 'privatized' away from the stock market, then 'IPOed'[45] a few months later, possibly through a leveraged management buy-out (LMBO).[46]

Although the exuberant activity of investment banks sometimes led to leverage excesses throughout the 1980s, they nevertheless deserve some credit for helping corporations or businesses increase their efficiency and profitability. It is not the least paradox of this time. At the end of the decade, however, the feeling was widespread that the sphere had grown into a bubble and that the uninterrupted rise of the financial markets since 1982 amounted to a form of inflation which was just the mirror of both others: price inflation on the one hand, debt inflation on the other. Three strong signals should, at the time, have drawn our attention to the increasing frailty of financial markets:

- Cracks from within the US banking system.
- The Crash of October 1987.
- Vulnerability of the largest market of the day: Tokyo.

Cracks from within the US banking system

This topic is too much developed elsewhere for us to dwell too long on it here.

Let us briefly examine some basic facts, however. In 1989, US banks underwent the quadruple pressure of the excessive debt load of some Latin American countries, of US households (the S&L problems), of US corporations (especially in the wake of the 1980s leverage craze), and finally of the US government (cumulated budget deficits). Once again, the economy had not taken on such a debt burden since the 1930s. It was thus particularly vulnerable to a possible growth slowdown. Savings banks in particular were the most vulnerable.

Until 1976, as a result of 'Regulation Q' putting a ceiling on interest paid to savers, the latter were not too badly treated since they obtained, on average, 60 basis points more on their deposits than the regular

---

[45] Resold back to the market through an Initial Public Offering.

[46] Leveraged Management Buy-out: the purchase of a company by its employees with very little equity capital and huge bank debt originally. Through subsequent secondary equity issues, the debt is quickly paid back.

Treasury-bill rate for a strictly equivalent risk, as these deposits benefited from the Federal Government's guarantee.

This constraint made it possible for the Federal Reserve to brutally close the mortgage valves through a modest increase in leading rates: new deposits immediately dried up in favour of Treasury bills. Deprived of new resources, savings banks immediately stopped granting loans.

The deregulation of deposits prevented the Federal Reserve from directly controlling the quantity of credit available. To achieve the same result, it now had to amplify the rise of its directing rates. According to certain observers, the record rise of interest rates observed in the period 1980 to 1981 (up to 20 per cent for the banking prime rate) had much to do with this phenomenon.

For our part, as faithful observers of Kondratieff's theory, we note that this peak in rates coincided with the inflation peak of 1980 to 1981, which looks consistent to us. Perhaps this deregulation was an instrument of the 'invisible hand' that led to price and rate increases.

In addition, it caused the construction cycle to become more volatile and transferred the rate risk to homebuyers, particularly after the introduction of variable rate loans (adjustable rate mortgages).

This last point is crucial, for it bore the seeds of the sizable real estate crash that struck the United States at the time of the Gulf crisis.

October 1987: missed rendezvous with history

The October 1987 crash was probably not the 'real' one, for two simple reasons: first, since the summer of 1987, the New York Stock Exchange had not been the world's leading exchange; second, since the total stock market capitalization of all exchanges at the end of 1987 was higher than at the end of 1986, it was not a real crash as there was no negative wealth effect[47] on the world as a whole. Even within the United States there was no negative wealth effect that year, firstly because the Stock Exchange still gained, albeit minimally (2 per cent), and secondly because the loss on equities due to the crash was largely offset by an upsurge in bond prices as a consequence of a 'flight to quality' syndrome.

---

[47] See article in *Le Figaro*, 15 December 1987.

It is still useful though to analyse the causes of the crash since this could be relevant for what was to follow. If we look strictly at the 'fundamental' causes of the crash, it can be seen as the result of not implementing the Louvre Accords in full. To explain, on 22 February 1987 the G7 met at the Louvre in Paris to review the benefits of the extensive economic and monetary cooperation which had been in effect since the September 1985 Plaza Agreement on the US dollar. Following this meeting, it was announced in a press release that all parties had agreed that:

- They would all stabilize the US dollar at around the then current level (6.1 French Francs).
- The United States would slow down consumption and stimulate production and exports.
- Europe and Japan would reduce exports and stimulate domestic consumption.

Although originally greeted with scepticism, the agreement nevertheless became the starting point for the strengthening of the financial markets until the summer. The Louvre proposals made it possible to count on a stable dollar, which revived confidence and led people to hope that the trade deficits could be rapidly wiped out. The markets lived on this fiction until the summer, the dollar reaching its height on 15 July and the Dow Jones a record high on 17 August.

Unfortunately, it was not long before disillusionment set in. US trade balance statistics for June, July and August, published in August, September and October respectively, revealed the following deficits:

June: US$15.6 billion
July: US$16.5 billion
August: US$17.6 billion

The markets realized that the Louvre Accords were just a myth when these figures were released at a time when Japan and Germany announced trade surpluses of unprecedented proportions. Confidence evaporated and the house of cards began to shake.

We must pause for a moment and look at the significance of the basic philosophy behind the Louvre agreements, whereby some countries were asked to reduce demand and stimulate supply, while others were summoned to do the opposite. It looks suspiciously like a cartel of producers dividing up world markets among themselves for lack of real growth. The analogy with the overproduction phenomena of the late 1920s is quite glaring.

In the days and weeks following the crash, Japan quickly emerged as a pillar of confidence upon which to rely, taking over as it were from the United States as the leading financial powerhouse. Remember, at the end of 1987 the Japanese stock market capitalization stood at over US$3000 billion, as compared to some US$2200 billion for the United States. Japan's tremendous financial supremacy led us to believe then that the next, real crash, if it came, would be ignited in Japan.

In the 1920s, the United States was vying for supremacy with Britain, just as Japan was vying with the United States in the 1980s.

Consequently, and it bears mentioning, a useful analogy could be made between, on the one hand, Japan in 1989 and the United States in the 1920s and, on the other, the United States in 1989 and Britain in the 1920s.

If this analogy were to hold true, the 1987 crash could be likened to the British stock market crisis of 1928, which preceded the crash of 1929 by only a few months. That is the reason why we felt that the 1987 crisis was only a missed rendezvous with history. There was to be another place and another time: Japan, two years later.

The vulnerability of the Japanese market

A few statistics will serve to highlight the exceptional fragility of the Japanese financial market on the eve of the Gulf crisis.

Stock market capitalization and GDP

Again, as at 31 March 1989, the Japanese stock market capitalization was approximately US$3900 billion compared with a GDP of US$2600 billion, ie. a ratio of 3:2. At the same date, the US stock market capitalization was US$2700 billion, compared with a GDP of US$4500 billion, ie. a ratio of 3:5. Per dollar of GDP, the Japanese stock market was thus two and a half times larger than the US stock exchange (a ratio of 5:2).

Price/earnings multiple

The average price/earnings multiple is commonly used to determine whether a stock market is relatively under- or over-valued. Let us assume that the price of a share in 'company x' is 100. If company x has achieved earnings per share of 10 during the past year and anticipates earnings of 12.5 during the current year, the price/earnings multiple is said to be 10 times for 1999 and 8 times for 2000. Since this multiple can be calculated for all companies quoted on a particular stock exchange, the average multiple for the exchange can also be calculated. The average price/earnings multiple on the New York Stock Exchange was expected to be in the region of 12.5 times as at 15 May 1989.

The average price/earnings multiple on the Tokyo Stock Exchange was some 60 times. Due to differences in accounting practices that resulted in a voluntary reduction in Japanese earnings, we could calculate an 'adjusted' multiple for the Tokyo Stock Exchange of approximately 25 times. If we compared this adjusted multiple with that of New York, we could measure the relative risk of Tokyo compared to Wall Street. If the Japanese multiple suddenly fell into line with its US counterpart (12.5 times), Japanese prices would be halved! We now know this is exactly what was to happen within a few years.

In fact, two main parameters determine the price/earnings multiple: the expected growth in earnings, 'g', and the interest rate, 'i'.

In general terms, the multiple is proportional to 'g' and inversely proportional to 'i'.

Note, incidentally, that the high Japanese multiples were consistent with the idea that growth was higher in Japan than elsewhere and that Japanese rates were lower than those of other countries (long-term rates of 5 per cent compared to 9 per cent in the United States in 1989). Consequently, two types of event could 'kill' the Japanese market:

- A rising tide of interest rates.
- A downscaling of growth prospects.

A steep increase in the dollar or price of oil, or both, would be enough to increase the cost of money in Japan. As for growth prospects, they would probably be downscaled during the next US recession. To the extent that these two parameters could be made to vary significantly, we had the seeds of a potential crash. While Tokyo appears in retrospect to have been an ideal candidate for the next crash, it was still possible that the spark would be lit elsewhere, in particular in the United States, given the cracks that then prevailed in the US banking system. The dramatic events which took place in early June 1989 in Beijing's Tiananmen Square led us to believe that other factors might also affect the sphere of Japanese co-prosperity: political instability in China, the destabilization of Hong Kong and the backlash effect on South Korea and Taiwan. By a curious coincidence, these events would have caught Japan by surprise at the worst possible time from a political point of view. For the first time since 1945, the governing party was racked by a deep crisis due to the Recruit Cosmos scandal, which had decimated its ranks and left it to all intents and purposes leaderless.

To sum up, the amazing parallel that we were able to draw between the 'roaring 20s' and the 1980s could be traced back to the same kind of debt-led financial speculation that was disconnected from reality because growth was not there anymore. In both cases the illusory euphoria of a few business circles had diffused deep enough into broad layers of the population to awake a generalized 'feel-good' sentiment, but it would have to end one day. Feel-good eras, bubble years – the euphoria felt is nothing but ephemeral.

6
The Crash of 1990 or Burst of the Japanese Bubble as a Resounding Echo of the Crash of 1929

The precedent parallel was so convincing that it did not fail to be recognized on the spot by some[48] and it was natural, at the end of the 1980s, and even if the consensus were resolutely hostile there, to raise the question of the possibility of a crash. This event was to constitute a crucial turning point, since in our model, and following the theories of Fisher, it led to the debt deflation era and in due course to a depression (or 'creative destruction', however you prefer to call it).

As we saw in Chapter 5, the day before the Gulf crisis, the financial sphere, for which Tokyo had become the blazing standard, was ripe for a fall. The US banking structure was fissured and the real estate and stock market bubble in Japan ready to burst. However, the idea of a crash was far from being unanimous, as if the public warning of October 1987, because it had had no impact whatsoever on the economy, had blunted the vigilance of all, commencing with the investors themselves. It should be noted that the business cycle was at its best and the Cassandras,[49]

---

[48] By a handful of well-advised investors, including notably Ed Hyman, then chief economist with Cyrus Lawrence, a brokerage firm later purchased by Deutsche Bank.

[49] Thanks to two interviews, one, by Anne Elisabeth Moutet, in *Fortune France*, March 1990, and the other by Liliane Galifet, *Paris Match*, 2 August 1990, the very day of Kuwait's invasion, we were lucky enough to publicize the threats that were looming over both our markets and economies. Let us express our gratitude to these two journalists, whose articles still bear witness to the validity of our foresight back then!

once more, were not listened to by the media, their point of view being too far removed from the official self-congratulatory statements.

At the time, when we considered the idea of a repetition of a scenario of the 1929 type, the main objection was the following: how to locate in time the calendar of the crash, the exact timing of the death knell? When one spoke about the long cycle, the margin of error appeared such over a duration of this kind that the predictions seemed extremely risky and daring. Such was in particular the objection of Philippe d'Arvisenet, then deputy-chief economist at the Banque Nationale de Paris. Thanks to him, we were able to sharpen our arguments around two lines:

- By analysing in detail the mechanics of the 'marvellous clock', we could isolate precisely both a critical zone and a margin of error, thus immensely reducing the random factor.
- By circumscribing the random factor down to the 'king's prerogative', the latter handling the stylet that pierces the bubble, we were able to find which king it was.

Marvellous precision of Kondratieff's clock: critical zone, margin of error and catalyst

Our stylized model developed in Chapter 1 is very precise while isolating and identifying the feel-good era as a prelude to the Crash and ensuing depressive phase. Under these conditions, the margin of error does not relate any more to the total duration of the cycle, but only to one of its phases, whose origin and end are clearly given: for the origin, the peak of prices (in fact, 1980) and for the end, the peak of debt; this last had been more difficult to ascertain in 1989 than the price peak, which had already been recognized for a few years in the collective memory and in economic textbooks. However, we had some leading hints that the debt peak was close, the first of which was that universal frailty of banking systems, and the levelling off of leveraged management buy-outs. Generally, we noted the progressive tightening of liquidity and credit, even more so in terms of *quantity* that in terms of *price* of money (ie. interest rate).

Margin of error and critical zone

When one spoke about predicting a major event of the long cycle, eg. a crash expected to reappear every 60 years, the principal objection focused on the margin of error over a duration of this kind. The argument had some merit and two types of phenomena appeared to give it credence:

1) The latest ascending phase of the price cycle 1940 to 1980 lasted 40 years, to compare with:

    25 years for the cycle 1789 to 1814
    20 years for the cycle 1847 to 1866
    25 years for the cycle 1896 to 1920.

Admittedly, one could say that World War II had probably cut short the price deflation of the preceding cycle, but the fact remained that the deviation from the average of the three cycles recognized by Kondratieff was statistically out of line.

2) Back in 1989, we had been flooded for at least a decade with a flurry of bestsellers predicting an incipient depression. Let us quote in particular: Paul Erdman, 'The Crash of 79', published in 1978; Robert Beckman, 'The Down Wave', edited in 1983, forecasting a depression for 1984; Ravi Batra, 'Depression of 1990', published in 1987.

This dispersion of predictions gave complete credence to the objection mentioned above. Nevertheless, our mechanistic model of the long cycle developed above looked set to bring forward a few brilliant counter-arguments.

Nobody could deny that the deceleration of world growth started in 1973, and the fact that the rate of world inflation began to decline in 1980 is well established. The two dates of 1973 and 1980 thus gave us undisputable markers of the downward phase of the cycle. It little mattered to us that the ascending phase of this same cycle was abnormally long. What was important from then on was the pattern of the downward phase.

Indeed, these two markers were perfectly pinpointing two areas of our model:

- The 'stagflation' phase of the plateau of the growth cycle, the inflationary stage par excellence. The duration of this phase was seven years, in comparison to:

  1807 to 1814: seven years
  1857 to 1866: nine years
  1913 to 1920: seven years
  Thus, this time, we were within the ballpark!
- The beginning of the feel-good era, corresponding to the second half of the plateau. Our model had listed three comparable periods:

  1814 to 1825: ten years
  1866 to 1873: seven years
  1920 to 1929: nine years.

Judging from the three preceding cycles, it followed that the 'normal' duration of a feel-good phase was about nine years. Thus, the margin of error should not be calculated relative to the total duration of the cycle, ie. 56 years, but should rather be viewed in the context of the sub-period that interested us, in other words approximately nine years. What it meant was that this margin of error was appreciably reduced, at least as long as the starting point of this sub-period could be clearly established: in this case, 1980. By estimating this margin of error at a generous 33 per cent, the 1986 to 1992 period could be estimated as the critical zone, with 1989 as the most probable year. Thus, the Japanese crash of 1990 came to put an end to this bubble phase *exactly in the ball park!* One will note, in addition, that it had been much a period of depression in 1986 when the price of oil collapsed in five months from US$28 to US$10 per barrel, and the price of gold fell to US$300. It will be also noted that the events of October 1987 were considered in retrospect as a serious warning, giving us confirmation that we were indeed in the critical zone.

The rise of over-indebtedness and the fact that public debt had started to become the major concern of most governments starting from the end of the 1980s were, without doubt, further hints to the relevance of our concept of the 'critical zone'.

But the problem from then on was the following: which catalyst within this critical zone was going to precipitate a crash, then a depression?

The answer to this question obviously lay with how the US business cycle was faring and how the US monetary authorities would manage it, for it was obvious that the next US recession would act as a trigger to this sequence of events. Were the Federal Reserve officials going to let the cycle die its natural death or, by opposing it, try to extend it to the maximum, through an undue fall in short rates?

The invasion of Kuwait by Iraq on 2 August 1990 hardly gave them a chance: an external, unforeseeable factor was going to simultaneously trigger a stock market crash in Tokyo and push the US economy into recession.

What would be the catalyst for the Japanese crash?

At the end of December 1989, the Nikkei index had reached an absolute record, as noted earlier. At the time, the yen was king and Japan the wealthiest country in the world. Indeed, was it not said that the commercial value (theoretical) of the Imperial Palace in Tokyo alone was equivalent to all of California? We saw earlier that the Japanese market capitalization was then 50 per cent higher than its US counterpart for a GDP twice smaller. This indecent health and wealth rested on the 'triple merit' formula of a strong yen, a weak oil price and the lowest interest rates in the world. At the beginning of February 1990, we analysed the Japanese market situation in the following terms, drawn from an interview with *Fortune France* dated March 1990.

Q: What do you think of the opinion that the Japanese market 'cannot fall'?
A: There is no such thing as a price that cannot fall. Today, a series of indicators demonstrates to us that Tokyo, already stagnant, can undergo a heavy correction in the coming months.

Q: Which indicators?

A: ... *the recent rise of long-term interest rates, from a low of 2.5 per cent in 1987 up to nearly 7 per cent last month* (they crossed the psychological threshold of 7 per cent on 26 January, to be maintained around 6.7 per cent approximately at the beginning of February). *The trend has little chance to be reversed, for the Bank of Japan, very worried by the fall of the yen, pushed the short rates above the 7 per cent mark. Let us not forget that the average PER in Tokyo is around 60 and the dividend yield is 0.5 per cent. As a consequence, the resistance of Japanese equities, already noticeable for some time, has started to falter. This move is likely to develop further.*

Q: Are there other reasons for a fall?

A: *Japanese corporations are the most leveraged in the world: the ratio of Japan's total debt reaches three times its GDP, while the United States is only at two. As long as interest rates were low, this debt was easily bearable. Today, that is no longer the case, which should slow down corporate investment and weigh heavily on corporate balance sheets. Finally, if the Japanese current account surplus amounts to US$60 billion annually, in the meantime, capital outflows reach twice as much or US$120 billion. Lately, the Japanese have indulged in what I will call the 'Grand Dukes' syndrome: factories, Picasso paintings, real estate – they buy everything, everywhere. That also means the Japanese saving surplus is not primarily focused towards corporations and that it is not inexhaustible.*

Q: Which position should be taken on the Japanese market?

A: *None. It is imperative to withdraw from all asset classes, be they equities, bonds or money market funds.*

Timing, the king's prerogative: but which king?

Thus, just before the Gulf crisis, the Tokyo market had started to drop under the pernicious influence of an increase in interest rates and of a sudden weakness in the yen. Naturally, the invasion of Kuwait in August accentuated these two phenomena while adding to them, for good measure, a third decisive blow to the 'triple merit' syndrome: the unexpected and brutal rise in the price of oil. From then on we had all the ingredients for a spectacular disarray of Japan Inc., and of the 'nouveaux riches' of the 1980s, who had so much indulged themselves in the Grand Duke rage: buying without counting a few jewels of US industry, but also Van Gogh and Picasso paintings at peak prices, not to mention a host of castles in Spain or France acquired amidst the euphoria at the top of the market, and which they would later be unable to maintain.

Given the extent of the world debt overhang that we have outlined at length in the previous chapter, it was clear to us in 1989 that the next business downturn would really turn the world economy upside down. For the leaders of the G7, the implicit questions that arose then should undoubtedly have been the following:

- Was there an ideal time to initiate the next recession, or allow it to take place, given that it could trigger a systemic crisis of world proportions?
- What would the ideal time look like?
- Wouldn't political considerations be of overriding importance in determining timing?
- Could the Kondratieff trap be avoided by seeking the positive effects of price deflation while minimizing its negative effects on volume decline?

The latter will be addressed separately in Chapter 7, in relation to stabilizers, and will single out Alan Greenspan's outstanding ability to tame the wave, so to speak.

But let us first tackle the others.

Was there an ideal time to trigger the crisis?

To respond to this question in depth would mean solving the problem of the origin of long cycles. Why are economic phenomena cyclical in nature? Our feeling was that the main cause of such cycles was both demographic and sociological, in the sense that the 'wealth and income distribution' problem led to age wave-related inflationary behavioural patterns, which in turn generated debt-fuelled speculative excesses and which had to be corrected in the end.

We then contented ourselves with taking a pragmatic approach, distinguishing between a pure business cycle play on the one hand, and a long cycle game on the other.

In the first context, the ideal timing from our point of view should have involved the least electoral considerations, in other words one that would respect the integrity of the natural business cycle. The situation was altogether different in the second case, for we could then ask: would it not, in fact, be worth delaying the onset of the crisis until we are fully prepared? In that sense, the ideal time would have been when society as a whole was fully prepared for deflation.

What would the ideal time look like?

The ideal time would have been when society was in a sufficiently advanced state of mental preparation to minimize the negative effects of price and debt deflation on business activity.

Back then, we thought it would have required a gigantic international cooperative effort and public awareness campaign to achieve the objective of minimizing unemployment, bankruptcies and imbalances. This appeared impossible at the time. Ten years ago, we thought a concerted effort to prepare society for deflation would not be politically acceptable. In retrospect, the United States has proved that the deflation taboo could be turned to the benefit of consumers and that a deflationary boom was feasible. Hence it is conceivable that humanity might one day reach such a degree of civilization as to find an elegant solution to the problem for all.

In any case, the world being what it was and still is, we knew the hour of truth would be determined by the way the US business cycle would be managed. At the time, there were three possible scenarios.

The first, the so-called 'natural death of the cycle', was the fastest way of leading into the crisis, but had the 'advantage' of moving its epicentre to Japan, which would then be the primary focus of any financial and real estate collapse.

The second, 'running before the storm', was an attempt to put off the fatal day as long as possible, on the principle that 'a bird in the hand was worth two in the bush'. However, this could have been a miscalculation, since financial markets were likely to become impatient over such delaying tactics and trigger a new crash fairly quickly, this time on US soil, from where the shockwaves would spread to Japan and the rest of the world.

Hence, it appeared then that the US authorities had very little room to manoeuvre, politically speaking. Even if they leaned towards a middle-of-the-road compromise between these two extremes, this could not protect them from a crisis in the near future – probably no later than by the summer of 1990.

To our greatest surprise, however, the 1990s gave the United States an opportunity to brilliantly illustrate how to adjust to a deflationary context while finding in themselves and in technical change enough energy to avoid a fall into depression. Thanks to exceptionally smart monetary and fiscal policies and to a liberal redefinition of the rules of

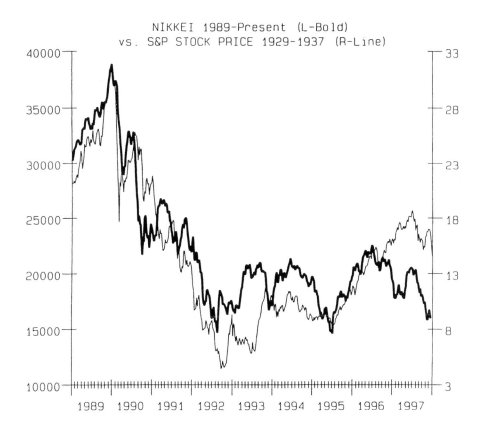

Figure 18. *A comparison between Tokyo (1989 to 1997) and New York (1929 to 1937) Stock Exchange indices*

the game, the country's 'vital forces'[50] could be unleashed and have growth spout out from a 'new virtual border': that of the information age. The United States found in the 1990s the means of mitigating for themselves the effects of a debt-led depression that started in fact in Tokyo. We largely see there the imprint of the Reagan revolution of the 1980s. Conversely, Japan did not foresee the brooding hurricane that threatened, proud as it was of its financial domination. Moreover, until the Gulf War, the timing of the next world recession remained in the hands of the man in charge of the US Federal Reserve System, Alan Greenspan.

Greenspan was anxious to save time and to gently delay the onset of the next business cycle recession, being satisfied with moderate rises in interest rates when an ordinary cycle would have required steeper ones. This 'prince of the business cycle' waited for his hour, hoping, no doubt confusedly, that New York would no longer be, as in 1929, the epicentre of the next seism, but that this 'privilege' be bestowed elsewhere. Another prince, from the oil world this time – in fact, Saddam Hussein – was going to implicitly fulfil this wish while triggering, even temporarily, the mini oil shock, which was going above all to penalize Japan.

Some Manichean spirits have recognized in this Iraqi move the Florentine hand of US diplomacy anxious to cast a severe blow to the large economic rival of the time. It is true that what happened to the Tokyo market in 1990 can be best described by the term 'crash' and that the climactic phase of the down wave, which we shall depict in Chapter 7, was especially prejudicial for Japan.

The crash of Tokyo was certainly spread out in time more than that of Wall Street in 1929, but it was no less brutal for that. An advanced warning signal of this had undoubtedly been given on 12 December 1989, three weeks before the effective record of the Nikkei index, by a fall of 200 points of the Dow Jones index on the news of the renouncement by Japanese banks to their share of United Airlines LMBO's financing deal. We had clearly interpreted this message as the awaited sign of the 'topping out' of Japanese debt and of the peak of the feelgood era for Japanese banks. Thereafter, the respective profiles of Nikkei in 1990 to 1997 and Dow Jones in 1930 to 1937 were very similar.

---

[50] Dr Arthur Laffer suggested 'animal spirits' here in this context.

It is thus on a comparative chart (see Figure 18) that we will close this parallel between Tokyo 1990 and New York 1929.

In short, what the 1920s and the 1980s had in common was the rising tide of debt and the financial speculation it nourished. Hence, it was natural, at the end of the 1980s, to raise the question of a potential crash, or bubble burst, immediately followed by a depression phase. As for the crash, we have just shown that Kondratieff's clock more than honoured its fateful date with history.

What about the post-crash era? The answer to this question forms the last stage of our demonstration, relying on that well-preset 'sequence of magnificent parallels' between the third scientifically recognized Kondratieff, which was completed in 1937, and the following cycle, of which we currently live the last moments of the down wave: such is at least our thesis. This last stage presents, however, an additional difficulty compared to the preceding ones: it is, essentially, a transitory stage, a double-faced one. On one side, it closes the depression of the preceding cycle; on the other, it announces the ensuing ascending wave. We find back here its function of 'destructive creation', which we earmarked in the prologue. This duality, although conceptually as inextricable as the Yin and Yang of Chinese philosophy, forces us, for the clarity of the demonstration, to operate in two steps.

Its negative or perverse aspects are treated as a mirror image of the crisis of the 1930s and can be viewed as the last item in our afore-mentioned checklist of 'magnificent parallels'. It is the purpose of the next chapter and allows us to validate the period 1973 to 1997 as typical of a Kondratieff's down wave. On the other hand, we will reserve its positive, fertile and visionary aspects for the third section, entitled 'Creative Destruction'.

From our analysis of the facts, we tentatively draw two conclusions, one major, the other minor.

The primary lesson is that the current decade indeed markedly qualifies as an echo of the 1930s. It is an important step in our demonstration, since it is the last item on our 'magnificent parallel' scheme. On the other hand, the second lesson is that this echo of the 1930s is a somewhat weakened echo: in short, the depression no longer is what it used to be. More than that: in fact the United States proved at length in the 1990s that depressions were avoidable. As Alan Greenspan put it, in his remarks of 13 January 2000:

'We are within weeks of establishing a record for the longest economic expansion in this nation's history. The 106-month expansion of the 1960s, which was elongated by the Vietnam War, will be surpassed in February. Nonetheless, there remain few evident signs of geriatric strain that typically presage an imminent economic downturn.'

What this amazing anomaly suggests to us is that depressions in the usual sense are nothing but 'worst case scenarios of destructive creation periods'.

7
Parallel Between the 1930s and the 1990s, or the Negative Aspect of this Ongoing 'Creative Destruction'

'One result of the more-rapid pace of IT innovation has been a visible acceleration of the process of 'creative destruction', a shifting of capital from failing technologies into those technologies at the cutting edge.

Indeed, the increasing availability of labour-displacing equipment and software, at declining prices and improving delivery lead times, is arguably at the root of the loss of business pricing power in recent years. To be sure, other inflation-suppressing forces have been at work as well. Marked increases in available global capacity were engendered as a number of countries that were previously members of the autarchic Soviet bloc opened to the West, and as many emerging-market economies blossomed.'

(Greenspan's speech before the Business Council,
Boca Raton, Florida, 28 October 1999)

Just as before the Gulf crisis, in the Summer of 1990 the world business cycle had started to deteriorate. In the United States, the yield curve had been briefly inverted around mid-1989, which was then viewed as an early warning of recession. Curiously, however, this time the slide into recession, observed one year later, was not accompanied by a hike in interest rates: on the contrary, and under the leadership of Alan Greenspan, who was then deeply concerned about the banking system, interest rates kept drifting downwards. Paradoxically, it was not reassuring in a context where the savings banks, and, subsequently, the whole banking system, were on the verge of collapse. In Japan, the fall of the Nikkei had begun in January 1990 due to a stellar rise in both short and long rates: the latter had reached 7 per cent on 26 January, which, in the context of over-leverage which hung over Japan Inc., was not a good omen. Let us recall that Japanese long rates had reached a low of 2.5 per cent in the summer of 1987. The rise of both the dollar and oil triggered by the invasion of Kuwait on 2 August 1990 only served to precipitate matters and worsen an already compromised situation. That event led to three further chains of event:

- First, it hurt with varying degrees the financial markets of the planet, Tokyo being hardest hit, due to its oil vulnerability.
- Second, it forced the United States into recession, in part due to an overall wait-and-see attitude caused by the threat of US military intervention in Iraq.
- Third, it led to massive price deflation in Tokyo, both of real estate and financial assets, thus opening the way to a true depression in Japan.

However, as time went on, it became clear that this depression differed from that of the 1930s in three ways:

- It was very focused on Japan, which from 1990 to 1998 embodied a rather exemplary illustration of Irving Fisher's debt deflation model.
- It marked an escalation in the gravity of the penalties endured depending on which zone was considered, Japan being hardest hit, then Europe, and then America.
- Until the Asian crisis erupted in 1997, it was softened overall by a variety of stabilizers.

The Japanese depression: illustration and textbook case of Fisher's model (1933)

What happened to Japan was exactly in line with economics textbooks describing Fisher's debt deflation logic as examined above. The fall of

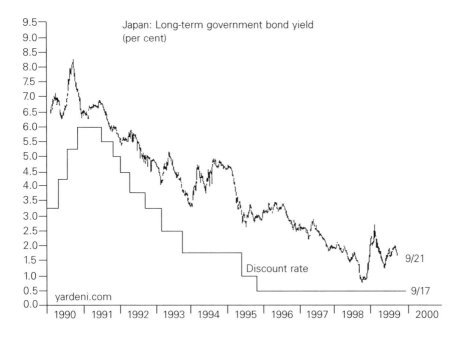

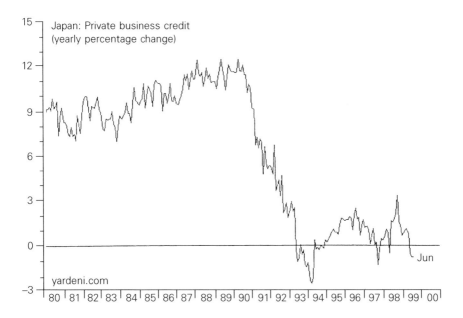

Figure 19. *Japanese deflation*

Source: Deutsche Morgan Grenfell Weekly Economic Analysis, 1999

equity and real estate assets beginning in 1990 weakened the Japanese banking system and reversed the process of monetary creation. This phenomenon is best illustrated by Figure 19, showing that Japan became a 'liquidity trap',[51] in the sense that efforts at monetary creation from the central bank, as attested by the fall near zero of short rates (top chart) were unable to instigate bank credit formation. Thus, no monies could find their way through the real economy (bottom chart).

This led the real economy to experience a prolonged stagnation from 1991 onwards, from which it had yet to emerge in 1999.

'Is Japan in depression?' asked Ed Yardeni, economist at Deutsche Morgan Grenfell, around mid-1995, only to assert at once: 'Certainly, for a depression is a recession which the authorities do not have the capacity to stop. The Japanese economy has been in the doldrums for more than two years in spite of aggressive monetary and budget stimulation policies. The strength of the yen, the deflation of assets and the banking crisis all depress economic activity'.[52] The central bank was very slow to appreciate the gravity of the situation: in the first months of the crisis, the Bank of Japan, while trying to support the yen for reasons of international credibility, felt obliged to accentuate its policy of monetary tightening at the worst time, while justifying its move by the desire to 'make the bubble burst' – as if the bubble would wait for permission before exploding! Meanwhile, Greenspan followed exactly the opposite policy in the United States, which enabled him to bail out the banking system in two years! Unfortunately, the Japanese central bank persisted in its error for at least two years, until the winter of 1992, which worsened the banking crisis, led to an over-valuation of the yen, and choked both the market and the economy. It took three years for monetary policy to be reversed, and it was not until the summer of 1995 that it became stimulative for real.

Figure 20 demonstrates the evolution of Japanese capacity utilization from 1980 to 1997. It took seven years for the index to re-achieve the 108 level last observed in 1991. This might sound like a remote echo of the Pharaoh's seven lean years, but it is even worse than it looks, as the

---

[51] According to JM Keynes' expression.
[52] Yardeni, E.: 'Weekly economic briefings', Deutsche Morgan Grenfell (1990–).

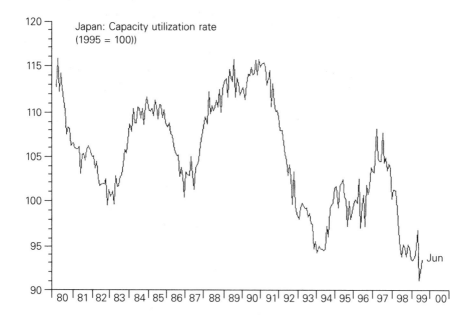

Figure 20. *Japanese industrial capacity utilization index 1990=100*

(Note this open bleeding hole in the index, for it has had no precedent since 1945)

index appallingly fell back in 1998. Overall, this industrial retrenchment qualifies as something much worse than an ordinary cyclical recession.

Figure 20 eloquently bears witness to the Japanese industrial depression of the 1990s. However, it was largely softened by the persistent dynamism of exports, in particular towards the United States and, lately, Asia.

Let us again stress that this trauma can best be traced back to a negative wealth effect of great proportions, ie. the stock market and real estate crashes of 1990. The latter themselves were an outgrowth of the debt overhang and excess leverage of the 1980s. To have an idea of Japanese over-indebtedness, it is enough to recall that from 1980 to 1989 the nation's large banks' balance sheets had increased by a factor of ten, at the same rate as the stock market rise. To give another example: at the end of 1989 Japan's total debt reached three times GDP, versus only twice in the United States. Before the crash, real estate prices had reached levels of about US$100,000 per m². Many Japanese households might at the time, while liquidating their mediocre dwelling in some dull Tokyo suburb, have secured for themselves high living standards forever in paradise spots around the globe without pausing to worry about the future: in the Pacific Islands, in Indonesia or even in Florida. In 1989 Ed Hyman, the US economist, quoted a Japanese fund manager, very far from being at the time at the top of his group's hierarchy, but who valued his flat at US$7 million, net of bank loans.

Of course, within Japanese society, even if the idea must have tempted some, such an act was unthinkable: for it would have been viewed as felony, happiness being conceived only inside woven social bonds in a feudal and immutable way. 'HMS Japan Inc.' had shaken the world to its foundations: she was going to sink with dignity, at least for all practical purposes. However, the collapse of the house of cards was going to unearth a wealth of scandals, which left a few scars within the once almighty liberal democrat party itself (they had been at the helm since 1945). It had to yield power to the socialist party of Mrs Do, then to various unworkable coalitions – signalling the end of an era.

Japanese society was thus wavering on its feet and losing its points of reference. At an industrial level, the large multinationals, which had built their competitive advantage partly on the very low cost of credit, from then on were caught by surprise by the rise in interest rates and the fall of the stock market. They had largely financed themselves through convertible bonds carrying almost no interest but with attached equity warrants. They hoped never to have to refund the principal, thanks to the anticipated appreciation of their stock price, which would have led the bondholders to exercise their warrants. In total, these issues had reached several hundred billion dollars, which were becoming difficult to refund in the depressive context of the 1990s. These financial difficulties were going to make those multinationals lose their technological lead in advanced industries: semiconductors, microprocessors, telecommunication equipment, health, medical etc. because of the over-investments carried out during the years of euphoria and which from then on were being under-utilized.

As supreme ignominy, in a roundabout way the Japanese government was instructed by Washington to provide the largest financial package, together with Saudi Arabia, for the 'Desert Storm' US war effort – a move Japan accepted perhaps as much with some secret pride as with hidden resentment.

In brief, if one were to find a Machiavellian interpretation to the Iraq crisis, perhaps we should ask whom 'had the crime objectively benefited' and whom, conversely, had it harmed most, apart from Kuwait and Iraq? The major crisis triggered by the Gulf War had not equally affected the industrialized world.

An escalation in the penalties incurred: Japan, Europe, United States

Of the three great rival economic zones, Japan was hit the most. Why? There are a number of clear reasons:

- Japan's real estate and financial bubbles of the 1980s had been the 'most exuberant' of all. Let us remember that, on the eve of the Iraq crisis, the Tokyo Stock Exchange was two and a half times more expensive than Wall Street, and real estate price excesses were incommensurable.
- As a consequence, Japan's asset deflation was also the most severe, with both the Nikkei index and real estate prices losing three-quarters of their value in three years.
- It took the Bank of Japan a very long time to recognize the acuity of the banking problems and to soften its monetary stance. Meanwhile, the budget and monetary policy mix supported an ill-fated appreciation of the yen, completely at odds with the US policy of 'benign neglect' with respect to the dollar. It was not until the summer of 1995 that the Japanese authorities became aware of their errors, their obsession with the bubble having misled them for many years.[53]

---

[53] While bubbles that burst are scarcely benign, the consequences need not be catastrophic for the economy.

The bursting of the Japanese bubble a decade ago did not lead immediately to sharp contractions in output or a significant rise in unemployment. Arguably, it was the subsequent failure to address the damage to the financial system in a timely manner that caused Japan's current economic problems. Likewise, while the stock market crash of 1929 was destabilizing, most analysts attribute the Great Depression to ensuing policy mistakes.' (Greenspan, 17 June 1999)

- The Japanese corporate fabric remained much more rigid than was the case in the United States or even Europe, especially in the retail sector and the financial sphere. The latter had to wait until 1 December 1998 for its 'big-bang' or deregulation. One can also mention cultural rigidities with regard to lay-offs, among others.
- Still being viewed as the champions of mass production, the Japanese apparently missed the technological turn of the 1990s in the field of high added value information systems, both for microprocessors and software services. (In addition, Europe also lagged behind.)
- The financial crisis shook the political world off its base, with a serious blow to the liberal democrat party, which had been a constant reference of Japanese political life since 1945; this trauma was accompanied by a true societal crisis leading to generalized existential introspection.

At the other end of the spectrum, the United States fared better through the crisis than their main competitors, and even largely benefited from it so as to assert their political and economic leadership. We suggest that this was the case for the following reasons:

- The US Federal Reserve System quickly implemented an expansionist monetary policy through a fall in leading rates and in the value of the currency to fight an early battle against brooding deflationary forces.[54] Thus, it was able to counter in due course the asset and credit deflation wave that later hit Japan so strongly. The temporary weakness of the dollar was a formidable asset in that battle.
- Although the real estate crisis was severe, the Dow Jones index fell only about 20 per cent from July to October 1990. From that base, the index increased fourfold in nine years, against a division by two and a half for the Nikkei over the same period.
- The Gulf War was a strong plus for the United States, while it harmed Japan:

---

[54] Contrary to what the bank of Japan did.

- The rise of oil prices relatively favoured the United States, while highly penalizing Japan.
- The financing of the war weighed heavily on Japan and Saudi Arabia, but very little on the United States.
- New markets were opened for the United States on this occasion, not only in the Middle East.
- The military outcome increased the prestige of America in the area and throughout the world.

- The new technological revolution proved an outstanding opportunity for the United States to regain control of leading edge technologies, such as microprocessors, computer software and many new age industries: in the field of aeronautics, defence, biotechnology, etc.
- The 'laissez-faire' policy with respect to international trade and the generalized fight against protectionism paid off: *this is perhaps the main difference from the 1930s.*
- The fall of the Berlin Wall and the Gulf crisis inaugurated the era of a new and undisputed 'pax americana' throughout the world, and onto the most extreme borders of traditional communist bastions. The arrogant prosperity of the dollar area in this phase of 'creative destruction' strongly underpinned US diplomatic positions in Asia, Latin America and even Africa.

As for Europe, it positioned itself somewhere between these two extremes, halfway between America and Japan. To start with, Europe was less involved in debt than Japan or the United States. Moreover, it initially benefited in business terms from the reunification of Germany, which played a powerful stimulating role at the beginning of the decade, at a time when North America was slipping into recession. The negative side of reunification was felt later, from 1992 onwards, in the following way:

- Through a strong rise in German indebtedness, which induced a prolonged tightening of the Bundesbank's monetary policy, triggering similar policies in other continental European countries, irrespective of their own economic situation

- . . . which eventually forced the whole area into a severe recession from September 1992 onwards, at a time when world deflationary forces were being unleashed and when...
- . . . the question of the timing of monetary union was being raised again, locking any possible budgetary easing and thus worsening social tensions within European Monetary Union (EMU) countries, which were bound by the Maastricht Treaty.

If Europe's case was never as severe as Japan's, partly because its banking structure was less fragile, the convergence requirements of the EMU agenda could not have materialized at a worst possible time from a long cycle perspective. By sheer coincidence, it happened that the last stretch towards the single currency had to take place within a recessionary and deflationary environment, which it would have been legitimate to counter through tax or interest rate cuts and by making the business climate more flexible. Unfortunately, the dogmatism of the Bundesbank proved very slow to adjust to a new environment. Because it crystallized the pride of the German people, it became the victim of what might be called the syndrome of the 'Bridge on the River Kwai'.

For didn't the Bundesbank become itself an object of worship? Did it in the end prove 'more credible' than the US Federal Reserve System, which in time became more flexible and finally more visionary? On the one hand, in the United States more than 18 million jobs were created in nine years and the rate of unemployment fell to 4.1 per cent in 1999 without inflation. Meanwhile, Europe still had creeping deflation and 17 million unemployed, more than 11 per cent of the working population.[55]

Yet, the example of Britain and the United States should have been food for thought for the central bankers of continental Europe and it should have brought them back to more modest thinking. One thing is certain: if the depression unequally struck the various countries, that was due partly to the different strategies that were led on behalf of central banks, but also partly to the influence of certain stabilizers.

[55] See former German Premier Helmut Schmidt's article in *Le Monde*, 9 November 1996: 'You exaggerate, Mr Tietmeyer'.

Influence of the stabilizers: is there such a thing as a 'soft depression'?

By stabilizer, we usually mean an automatic mean reverting force – such as unemployment compensation programmes – but the concept can also encompass ad hoc economic policy adjustments, or fine tuning moves aimed at smoothing business cycle excesses and preparing for a quick reversal.

Example 1: In the overheating phase, the tightening of monetary policy cools off outstanding excesses and opens the way for the subsequent recession.

Example 2: In the recession phase, the easing of budget policy makes it possible to soften the rigours of unemployment and kick-start the engine again.

However, within the framework of the long cycle, and in particular within the stage of 'creative destruction', there is no way that 'business cycle stabilizers' can do their usual job. Moreover, as we noted above, given the two evils responsible for the end of the up wave resulting from the abandonment of both monetary and budgetary disciplines, a Keynesian move par excellence, it would be paradoxical to resort to Keynes to cure the very excesses of his own pharmacopoeia. In Japan especially, a sequence of expansionist budget policies was implemented year after year to try to kick-start business activity again; in spite of the huge amounts of money involved, their impact proved similar to a trickle of water trying to irrigate huge desert sand tracks.

This is because only structural stabilizers can be effective within this kind of framework.

In an internal memo of a large bank, we wrote in a premonitory way in June 1989: 'If a problem deserves to be raised at the world level within the economic directory of the G7 group, it must be this one: how to cope with price and debt deflation while minimizing its influence on business activity? Within conventional wisdom, the confusion is so deeply enrooted between the concepts of deflation and depression that the long wave specialists themselves have not always succeeded in clearing up the matter'.

However, in a certain way, our wish was fulfilled due to the relative softness of the depression of the 1990s compared with the 1930s, at least in terms of growth. With regard to the behaviour of the US economy, one could even speak of an arrogant provocation. How to account for this success if not through the emergence of structural stabilizers?

We have earmarked four of them:

- The redistribution of economic power within the OECD in a free trade context.
- The rising wave of liberalism.
- The crucial role of the greying age wave within the richer countries.
- Lessons from the 1930s that only the United States seems to have learnt.

The redistribution of economic power in a free trade world

From 1945 to 1980, the United States had been the unique leading and attracting focus within the constellation of the richer countries. Their crushing weight compared to the rest of the world had given America an unquestioned driving role. The progressive emergence of Japan, on the one hand, and of Europe, on the other, has broken the celestial mechanics, which centred on a single economic sun, to substitute for another, based on three driving engines, and which we might label tri-polar – at least until another configuration emerges of a multipolar nature. This new balance of power has proved more beneficial than harmful. On the positive side, the dispersion of the sources of growth and their possible de-synchronization have secured lesser volatility in world output growth. In addition, by levelling off status differentials between partners, this rebalancing has proved a catalyst for increased dialogue between industrial powers. Hence the consistent success of those periodic meetings of the G7, recently promoted to G8 since the Summit of Denver of June 1997, with Russia joining in with observer status.

For its part, Japan, while being promoted to a fully-fledged regional power, has attracted in its trail a myriad of Asian countries that it has helped to awaken from under-development – Taiwan and South Korea in particular. Capitalizing on its new financial wealth, Japan assumed, on the eve of the Gulf crisis, an increasing share in the financing of US deficits and of international assistance to the most leveraged among Third World countries.

As for Europe, it had no other choice but to accelerate its making along a difficult but promising route, where the deadline of the single currency in 1999, and the prospects for its enlargement to the east seemed to shine in the distance like path–illuminating lighthouses.

That this worldly redistribution of the cards within the richer countries had reassuring sides was not to be questioned. These positive aspects, however, should definitely not have concealed the other side of the coin, ie. pitiless competition between these three zones in their search for commercial outlets. In one way, the rise of Japan was achieved to the detriment of the United States, whose weaknesses it had learned to exploit, at least until the Gulf crisis. For one should not forget that in recent years US external imbalances have had very focused counterparts: these have been and still are the Japanese and now Chinese surpluses.

However, as long as the recycling of commercial surpluses was carried out smoothly, the balance of the world was preserved. Besides, and it is perhaps one of the greatest achievements of Ronald Reagan, the banning of protectionism on a world scale had increased the chances of keeping an equilibrium over time that would no longer be static, but dynamic instead.

In this new paradigm, commercial imbalances were neutralized by financial flows in the opposite direction, which were fostered by the globalization of the markets.

There is no doubt that the generalization of free trade to the whole world has been one of the major structural stabilizers of the transition of the 1990s.

'It is safe to say that we are witnessing this decade, in the United States, history's most compelling demonstration of the productive capacity of free peoples operating in free markets. I said earlier this year that members of the graduating class of 1999 are being bequeathed the tools for achieving a material existence that neither my generation nor any that preceded it could have even remotely imagined as we began our life's work.'

(Alan Greenspan, Grand Valley State University & Ford Museum
Millennium Lecture Series, 9 September, 1999)

The wave of liberalism

With the 20th century drawing to a close, the rising wave of liberalism, which so much invigorated the Anglo-Saxon countries, and of which Ronald Reagan was the perfect symbol, spread to the rest of the world, but did not confine itself to the West. Indeed, just as before the fall of the Berlin Wall, the communist bloc, in perfect sync, had started to open its arms to it. From Communist China to the then Soviet Union, not to mention Vietnam and Cuba, the power of 'perestroïka' (restructuring) was so strong at the time of the Gulf crisis that the possibility of an effective disappearance of Communism before the year 2000 then appeared highly likely. The fall of the Berlin Wall would accelerate the pace of history, thus opening new outlets – and also new competitors – to the capitalist world. By codifying in an empirical way the interactions between the real world and the financial sphere, the liberal wave unleashed an unexpected flood of privatizations in countries up to then closed to any stock market logic. Hence it substituted the logic of debt financing for an equity funding philosophy. While unleashing the 'animal spirits' that had been kept in check by the yoke of interventionism, it gave chance to the entrepreneurial drive. Being the champions of financial engineering, and supported by this irresistible wave, the Anglo-American investment banks found in this crusade an unexpected vector of long-term growth. It is rumoured that the City of London and all related activities are a dominant force within British GDP, weighing around 20 per cent of the total. But this geographical extension of liberalism coincided with the emergence of an ascending cycle of newly industrialized countries.[56]

---

[56] One may wonder at length whether there is only one Kondratieff cycle, and raise the issue of a temporary configuration (by 'temporary', though, we mean a few years, a decade . . . a breather over such a large scale!), whereby two long cycles would simultaneously co-exist: a central one for the leading countries, then on their down wave, and a secondary up wave for emerging areas. That configuration would perfectly fit with the 1990s, which bears witness, as will be explained in Chapter 10, of the progressive rise of both Southeast Asian and Latin American economies. In fact, since the beginning of this decade, about one half of world GDP growth can be traced back to newly industrialized countries.

This is why the extension of liberalism and the concomitant financiarisation of whole chunks of continents, which had been closed until then to capitalist logic, permitted, in conjunction with the rise of emerging countries, an effective backfire to the underlying depression/deflation forces that have plagued the industrialized countries from the 1990s to today.

The role of a greying age wave

It is no secret for anybody that industrialized countries are ageing quickly, that the active age brackets are increasingly hollow, and that the retired population is in strong expansion. In the long run this situation is not favourable, in particular in light of the next ascending phase of the Kondratieff cycle of 2000 to 2030. In the short term, however, these numerous older generations with their strong saving potential provide an opportunity for the stock market, given their recurring appetite for equities. In the United States, the papyboomers' strive for equity pension funds of the 401K[57] type must probably be viewed as a prime mover in the 1990s flight of the New York market, despite an overall 'creative destruction' environment worldwide.

This is the reason why demographic trends constituted a crucial stabilizer, of obvious structural nature, for the financial markets of the 1990s.

Lessons of the 1930s, for the great benefit of the United States

That the United States could fare so well through the depressive phase of the 1990s, compared to Japan and Europe, undoubtedly lies with an early comprehension by Alan Greenspan of the deflationary threat.

On this last point, we wonder whether the head of the Federal Reserve System was not the only central banker on earth to have learned the lessons of the 1930s, especially in the framework of Irving Fisher's theories. You must judge for yourselves:

---

[57] 401K type pension funds: refers to US regulations on pension funds.

Stock prices behaved similarly in the initial phase of the 1929 and 1987 crashes, but a different response by monetary authorities entailed very different developments in both equity prices and aggregate output following the initial crises.

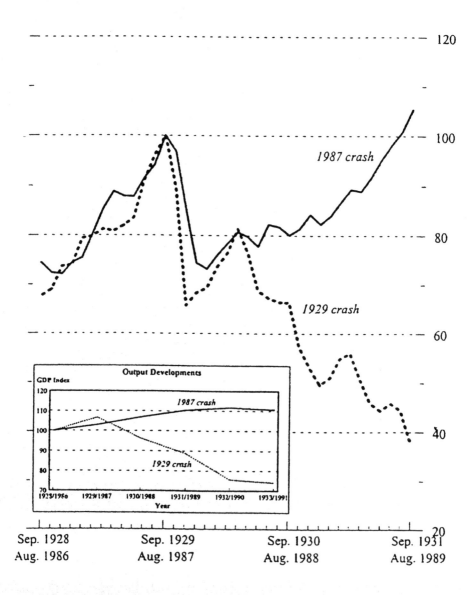

Figure 21. *Comparison of Two Stock Market Crashes*

Source: IMF Bureau of Economic Analysis, *Business Conditions Digest*; and IMF, WEO database.

In Fisher's terms

> '. . . in the great booms or depressions, two factors dominate, namely
> over-indebtedness to start with and deflation following soon after
> . . . and where any of the other factors do become conspicuous,
> they are often merely effects or symptoms of these two. In short,
> the big bad actors are debt disturbances and price level disturb-
> ances . . . Disturbances in these two factors, debt and the purchasing
> power of money, will set up serious disturbances in all, or nearly
> all, other economic variables. The depression out of which we are
> now (I trust) emerging[58] is an example of a debt deflation depression
> of the most serious sort. The debts of 1929 were the greatest known,
> both nominally and in truth, up to that time. They were great
> enough to not only 'rock the boat' but also to start it capsizing. By
> March 1933, liquidation had certainly reduced the debts about 20
> per cent, but had increased the dollar about 75 per cent, so that the
> real debt, that is the debt as measured in terms of commodities,
> was increased about 40 per cent'.

Fisher concluded,

> 'If the foregoing analysis is correct, it is always economically possible
> to stop, or prevent such a depression, simply by re-inflating the
> price level up to the average level at which outstanding debts were
> contracted by existing debtors and assumed by existing creditors,
> and then maintaining that level without change. The fact that
> immediate reversal of deflation is easily achieved by the use, or
> even the prospect of use, of appropriate instrumentalities, has just
> been demonstrated by President Roosevelt. Those who think that
> Roosevelt's avowed re-inflation is not the cause of our recovery
> but that we had reached the bottom anyway, are very much
> mistaken'.

Let us replace Roosevelt with Greenspan and there we have it.

The outstanding expertise that the United States has shown in handling
its debt overhang of the early 1990s thus largely contributed to moving
away the spectrum of an economic trauma 'à la 1930s'.

---

[58] That is, in 1933.

A sequence of magnificent parallels

If the Tokyo Stock Market crash of 1990 is the mirror image of New York 1929, the comparison then quite naturally shifts towards both post-crash eras. Japan being now the epicentre of the seismic wave, this time we focus our projector away from the stock market towards the banking system – the obvious bridge between finance and the real world. There again, the parallel proves striking between the present distress of large Japanese city banks, whose equity capital found itself crushed by their volume of non-performing loans, and the depositors' run on US banks in the 1930s. The great difference between the two periods lies with much greater support from central banks nowadays and the fact that no panic behaviour on behalf of the households was observed this time.

The central banks' cold-blooded attitude this decade has made it possible to very quickly counter the deflationary spiral of asset destruction through policies of massive monetary stimulation. Hence, it was possible to avoid any contraction of the money supply and the disastrous effects that would have resulted on the real economy. From this point of view, the lesson of the 1930s was heard, and Japan itself, although the true epicentre of the seismic shock, has not experienced a depression of the usual kind: ie. several consecutive years of recession. But one could speak instead of a revolving recession affecting successively whole chunks of the economy, especially in the industrial sector (see Figure 20, page 91).

If the depression has proven mild from a real growth standpoint, the G7 countries, on the other hand, have been largely exposed to the deflationary forces that have shaken the industrial world since the Tokyo crash. As a prime witness to these obscure forces, the technology sector has experienced continuous drops in prices together with simultaneous improvement in real performance. Price deflation has unfortunately also affected traditional industries, which were not prepared to meet the challenge of unrestrained Asian competition, which in turn has worsened unemployment.

From an unemployment point of view, Europe will probably have been the main loser in this down wave, because, apart from Japan, it proved the most reluctant to move towards social flexibility.

In Europe, at least, the trauma of unemployment has been a common, albeit softened, feature with the 1930s.

Finally, even if the lessons of the 1930s were eventually taken into account, especially on the US side of the Atlantic, making it possible to dampen the effects of the Japanese crash on the rest of the world, the similarities are no less remarkable between the two periods. In both cases we experienced banking crises, deflationary pressures, larval recession and more or less unemployment depending on the countries involved.

Finally, we dare to say that the 1990s rightfully qualify as an echo of the 1930s, which, in turn, validates the whole 1973 to 1997 period as typical of a Kondratieff down wave.

Our work is almost complete. We have yet to explore the potential benefits of the current destructive phase, hence the fruitfulness of this 'creative destruction'.

PART THREE

CREATIVE DESTRUCTION OR THE POSITIVE SIDE OF DEPRESSION

Soft you now, the fair Ophelia (Hamlet, Act III, 3)

'When we look back at the 1990s, from the perspective of say 2010, the nature of the forces currently in train will have presumably become clearer. We may conceivably conclude from that vantage point that, at the turn of the millennium, the American economy was experiencing a once-in-a-century acceleration of innovation, which propelled forward productivity, output, corporate profits, and stock prices at a pace not seen in generations, if ever.'

(Alan Greenspan, 13 January, 2000)

8
The Depression Myths and Realities: Fruitfulness of the Depression

'The quintessential manifestations of America's industrial might earlier this century – large steel mills, auto assembly plants, petrochemical complexes, and skyscrapers – have been replaced by a gross domestic product that has been downsized as ideas have replaced physical bulk and effort as creators of value. Today, economic value is best symbolized by exceedingly complex, miniaturized integrated circuits and the ideas – the software – that utilize them. Most of what we currently perceive as value and wealth is intellectual and impalpable.

The American economy, clearly more than most, is in the grip of what the eminent Harvard professor Joseph Schumpeter many years ago called "creative destruction", the continuous process by which emerging technologies push out the old. Standards of living rise when incomes created by the productive facilities employing older, increasingly obsolescent, technologies are marshalled to finance the newly produced capital assets that embody cutting-edge technologies.

This is the process by which wealth is created, incremental step by incremental step. It presupposes a continuous churning of an economy as the new displaces the old. Although this process of productive obsolescence has ancient roots, it appears to have taken on a quickened pace in recent years and changed its character. The remarkable, and partly fortuitous, coming together of the technologies that make up what we label IT – information technologies – has begun to alter, fundamentally, the manner in which we do business and create economic value, often in ways that were not readily foreseeable even a decade ago.'

(Remarks by Chairman Alan Greenspan, 'Maintaining Economic Vitality', Millennium Lecture Series, 8 September, 1999.)

Once again, the concept of depression is double-faced, with its ominous side finding its mythical dimension in its destructive instinct: the crash of 1987 was for us, as actors on the world financial stage, the opportunity to really feel its ghost linger around for the first time.

On the contrary, its other face is smiling and serene, for a depression bears with it its own contradiction, ie. revival.

Depression as a myth

Mystery and myth surround this concept and its content is almost as emotional as war, which is even more of a taboo. In fact, it is a concept as old as war if one believes in Pharaoh's dream in the Bible, with its seven years of fatted cows followed by seven lean years. In addition, it is an experiment one usually goes through only once in a lifetime, since its periodicity is about two generations (60 years). This is why it is a test that one generally goes through without being prepared for it. For those of us who did not live through the depression of the 1930s, the advent of an ordeal of this nature remained theoretically conceivable but most definitely impalpable.

The crash of October 1987 opened our eyes. The whole investment community can bear witness to this. Not until 19 October 1987 had a repetition of the crash of 1929 seemed possible. And yet, the fall in prices that occurred that day on Wall Street (−22.9 per cent) was about twice as bad as that of 1929 (−12.9 per cent), relegating it to backstage acting. All those who took part in that fatal session,[59] or followed it online from their screens, have shared the same complex pallet of feelings. Stupor

---

[59] The author included.

initially: 'worse than 1929', then the secret pride of attending the fall of a myth, while bearing witness to the birth of another; and also the rare feeling of living some unique moment. Lastly, an appalling anxiety dawning upon one, with the prospect of imminent recession, falling prices, the rise of unemployment and bankruptcies.

This anguish quickly dissipated though, due to the swift and smart reaction of the Federal Reserve System which decided to provide all the liquidities needed: 'Fed buys all notes'.[60]

And as, in the meantime, the Tokyo Stock Exchange, which had grown to number one market cap in the world as of July, had kept perfectly cold-blooded, one very quickly felt that the end of the world had not yet arrived.

Thereafter, the excellent performance of the world economy in 1988 did little to keep alive the vigilance that had been temporarily awakened by the warning signal of 19 October 1987.

'History usually gives no advance warning,' says one. However, the warning of 1987 was premonitory, for it announced a double shockwave two years in advance: the fall of the Berlin Wall and the collapse of the Soviet Empire on the one hand,[61] the outburst of the real estate and stock exchange bubbles in Tokyo on the other. This is the reason why the 1990s were clearly marked by a crawling depression both in Japan and Russia, not forgetting Soviet bloc countries. Western Europe itself felt the wind of the bullet, and Asian countries, more still.

---

[60] Literally: the Central Bank bids for all notes around, which means an exceptional injection of liquidity into the system. We might say: flooding the market with cash.

[61] To justify this prophecy, let us recall that 1987 was marked both by rising financial business in the United States, and by a decisive breakthrough for Mr Gorbachev's 'perestroika'. Witness the first intrusions that year in Moscow of US investment banks, and a series of surprising 'ads' in the *Wall Street Journal* from Soviet conglomerates. These early hints reflected in their own way the advance state of decay of the Soviet economy, which can be viewed in retrospect as the primary cause for the fall of the Berlin Wall in October 1989. Can the Russian depression of the 1990s be accounted for by some over indebtedness or excess leverage? In any case, it did not happen then by pure chance: did the 1917 October Revolution eventually get caught up by Kondratieff? Some post mortem revenge may be at stake here, together with promising doctoral dissertations in sight . . .

To put the concept of depression into perspective, let us return to the theory of the long cycle. In Chapter 1, we described its various phases, noting also that the periods of expansion lasted much longer than the depressions, by a factor of ten. Hence, the duration of a depression is approximately six years out of sixty for a complete cycle.

In terms of cumulated effects, depressions destroy only a small portion of the wealth put aside during the times of expansion that precede them. Their negative role is thus confined to slowing down, but not stopping, the process of capital accumulation that continues unabated from one cycle to another. The price to pay for the regulation of the cycle remains overall relatively limited, even if the brutality of the phenomenon makes it painful to the economic agents. However, the excesses made during the growth phases call for a regulating mechanism.

A regulatory function

Depressions proceed from a creative destruction impulse whose purpose is to clean the system of its past excess leverage, to possibly renew the rules of the game, to initialize meters back to zero, to prepare for the technological and psychological renewal of the following up wave, and, finally, to open the geographical field of development to a new set of countries.

To clean the system of its excess leverage

Lengthy growth periods generate, after a certain time, inflationary behaviours, for reasons related to wealth and income distribution: between capital and labour, between retirees and the working population, between the public and the private sectors. Initially, inflation softens the tensions, then exacerbates them. In turn, the inflation wave produces another poison: debt, insofar as each one understands that all it takes to get rich is to be involved in debt – on the condition of 'being able' to borrow.

However, inflation and debt end up choking real growth and the social body engages in a disinflation policy: aimed at dampening prices initially and at controlling debt later.

It is this very process of debt deflation that is the most painful, for it goes through asset disposals at large discounts to their face value. Debt deflation is thus the prime mover of depressions.

Hence the regulating role of depressions appears clearly established, in particular by resetting the balance between debtors and creditors, the latter being hurt during inflationary phases and the former during deflation.

To renew the rules of the game

So, if one of the causes for depression exists in the excessive concentration of financial assets in a small number of hands[62] and in the relative impoverishment of the greatest number, it would seem that depressions contribute to a more democratic redistribution of the cards (New Deal), at the same time coinciding with a more 'socialist' vision of economic problems (Keynes against Friedman).

This almost Marxist approach to depression, which would have fitted well within Kondratieff's initial mandate with the Gosplan,[63] applies rather well to the situation of the 1930s. Let us remember that the situation at the time was heavily worsened by the generalization of protectionism, but this approach looks completely out of date today, at a time when the role of governments is called into question almost everywhere, including Russia and China.

In the United States, it is true that a process of democratic redistribution of the cards is happening, but it is as a result of increasing individual stock-ownership and President Reagan's liberal revolution. The wave of LMBOs, an extraordinarily effective modern form of stock exchange speculation conceived originally for the benefit of a small number, saw its diffusion extending to increasingly broader employee numbers.

Let us give a striking example of an LMBO using Rexene, formerly the chemical division of a leading industrial group. In March 1988, a

---

[62] Batra, R.: 'The Great Depression of 1990', Simon & Schuster, New York, 1987.

[63] Let us recall here that Kondratieff's initial research was made under Gosplan's guidelines. However, his conclusions were viewed as reactionary or deviant: far from predicting the end of capitalism, he saw it cyclically rebound from its ashes. Hence, Kondratieff was sent to the gulag and sentenced to death in 1938.

small group of executives of the company purchases Rexene for US$600 million: their initial setting is US$6 million only, the balance being financed by banks. Four months later, this small group sells back on the market 20 per cent of their initial capital for US$200 million. What a splendid juggling act and what a gold mine for the initiators of this financial transaction!

Today, it is likely that such an operation would be realizable only if it involved most of the employees, and from a resolutely industrial point of view.

This is why the so-called 'impoverishment wave' affecting part of the US population should be viewed in perspective with such a low rate of unemployment (4 per cent in December 1999) and such a high rate of individual stock-ownership: approximately 100 million people are shareholders in the United States, where some blue collars have attained millionaire status.

Fruitfulness of the depression

To prepare for the technological change of the next up wave

Information has become the raw material par excellence of our mutant economies. We can never stress enough that it is absolutely the norm that a phase of price deflation be accompanied by a technological revolution and that the two phenomena reinforce one another. Indeed, technical progress changes the rules of productivity by building a new supply schedule of goods and services, shifted from the old one at lower prices. In their time, the preceding technical revolutions also coincided with price deflation eras: spinning mills and textiles under Louis XVI, railways under Queen Victoria, industrial chemistry *c.*1895 at the onset of the 'Belle Epoque'. However, it is the microprocessor revolution and the explosion of the Internet that today give us the brightest illustration of all. From now on, we have the feeling that a growing share of human activities, and thus of the GDP of each country, will be forwarded through information superhighways. Even a field as steeped in tradition as medicine seems today to be caught up by the twinned information age and biotechnology revolutions.

In Alan Greenspan's words, we are going through another industrial revolutions:

'Since the dawn of the industrial revolution, there has been an inexorable drive to leverage physical brawn and material resources into ever-greater value added or output. New insights into the laws of nature brought steam and later electric power. The development of precision production standards that facilitated interchangeable parts brought assembly-line production. And the development of railroads facilitated the evolution of mass markets.

Almost all the rise in value added relative to physical input has reflected the substitution of ideas – new insights – for brute human effort and material bulk. Some of the most impressive advances in labour productivity over the decades have come in sectors of the economy in which physical effort was the most demanding – agriculture, for example. Aggregate value added by the farm sector has more than tripled in real terms over the past half-century, but the number of hours required to produce it has fallen by three-fourths. Manufacturing has displayed similar, though less pronounced, tendencies in recent decades – factory employment is down about 13 per cent from its peak of twenty years ago, but output of the sector has risen about 75 per cent.

Like labour inputs, material requirements per unit of output also have fallen in many sectors of the economy. The insights of metallurgy and architectural and engineering design, for example, enabled the construction of buildings that use far less physical material per unit of space than, say, a half-century ago. The insights that led to central heating, as well as synthetic fibre, facilitated reduced clothing weight, while the development of the jet engine brought far greater annual passenger miles per unit of aircraft size.

But doubtless it has been the advent in recent decades of the synergies of the microprocessor, lasers, and fibre optics that has fostered a distinct quickening in the displacement of physical weight of output with concepts. The ability to miniaturize transistor electronic circuits has displaced huge tonnages of copper and enhanced the speed of calculation.

As high tech became an increasing part of our national product, the relative physical dimensions of our value added fell dramatically. The per capita physical weight of our gross domestic product is evidently only scarcely higher today than it was fifty or one hundred years ago. By far the largest contributor to growth of our price-adjusted GDP, or value added, has been ideas – insights that leveraged physical reality. The consequent downsizing of output, of course, meant that products were easier, and hence less costly, to move . . .'

(Remarks by Chairman Alan Greenspan, 'Trade and Technology',
Before the Minnesota meeting, Minneapolis, Minnesota,
30 September, 1999)

Also, on the information age:

'Before the advent of what has become a veritable avalanche of information technology innovation, most twentieth-century business decision making had been hampered by dated and incomplete information about customer preferences in markets and flows of materials through a company's production systems. Relevant information was hours, days, or even weeks old. Accordingly, business managers had to double up on materials and people to protect against the inevitable misjudgements that were part and parcel of production planning. Ample inventory levels were needed to ensure output schedules, and backup teams of people and machines were required to maintain quality control and respond to unanticipated developments.

Of course, large remnants of imprecision still persist, but the remarkable surge in the availability of real-time information in recent years has sharply reduced the degree of uncertainty confronting business management. This has enabled businesses to remove large swaths of now unnecessary inventory, and dispense with much programmed worker and capital redundancies. As a consequence, growth in output per work hour has accelerated, elevating the standards of living of the average American worker.

Intermediate production and distribution processes, so essential when information and quality control were poor, are being bypassed and eventually eliminated. The proliferation of Internet web sites is promising to alter significantly the way large parts of our distribution system are managed. Moreover, technological innovations have spread far beyond the factory floor and retail and wholesale distribution channels. Biotech, for example, is revolutionizing medicine and agriculture, with far reaching consequences for the quality of life not only in the United States but around the world.

The explosion in the variety of products of many different designs and qualities has opened up the potential for the satisfaction of consumer needs not evident even a decade or two ago. The accompanying expansion of incomes and wealth has been truly impressive, though regrettably the gains have not been as widely spread across households as I would like.'

(Remarks by Chairman Alan Greenspan, 'Maintaining Economic Vitality', Millennium Lecture Series, 8 September, 1999.)

To open new grounds for development

As a result of the depression phase of the 1990s and the fall of Communism, the field of development has opened up to new geographical areas: China, Vietnam and India are the next candidates in line to join the ranks of newly industrialized countries, in addition to Brazil, Mexico and others. Even the Asian crisis, as serious as it may be, won't stop the momentum. As for Russia and her former satellites, their turn will also come. The same can be said for Africa.

Every cloud has a silver lining (or Seeds of the rebound in creative destruction)

We are probably living through the last jitters of a long down wave which began in 1973 in the wake of the abandonment of the monetary discipline of Bretton Woods and which worsened in the 1980s through the rise of over-indebtedness on a worldwide scale. The major financial jolts of the 1990s (eg. the Tokyo crash, the US savings banks collapse, the worldwide real estate and banking crisis, etc) caused a backlash on the real economy by opening an era of creative destruction, according to Schumpeter.[64] A prolonged industrial recession both in Japan and continental Europe (not forgetting the former Soviet bloc countries), the rising threat of international competition, the shock of deregulation and technological change, the rise in unemployment combined with crawling deflation and the growing weight of debts, and the restrictive influence that vigilant budget policies had on business activity, were a rather good mirror image of the 'destructive' side of these 1990s. What was less visible, though, was that this sequence of events carried in itself the seeds of its own denial, ie. revival.

The debt overhang of our economies – and the deflationary threat it implied – called for policies that favoured de-leveraging through privatizations and lower public spending. It also led to 'reflationary' monetary policies (through lower interest rates and liquidity injections), and to stimulative fiscal policies (through tax cuts), which helped foster structurally sound recoveries.

Excesses of the Welfare State meanwhile triggered the correcting response of the liberal revolution, which, since the fall of the Berlin Wall, has spread to the whole world. It acted as a catalyst for growth by unleashing individual initiatives and energies. It substituted the comfort of welfare for an entrepreneurial spirit, an interventionist bias for a free enterprise stance, and leverage logic for equity funding dynamics.

It is from within the disarray brought about by technological change that the information age was born in the industrialized countries, opening up for them new avenues for growth, which, combined with the catch-up thrust of nations such as China, India or Brazil, will be the prime movers of a new 30-year up wave.

Are the Asian crisis of summer 1997, the Russian default of 1998 and the Brazilian jitters of early 1999, not to mention a prolonged Japanese recession, the final obstacle to this advent? On the contrary, we believe that they all take part in this fertile process of creative destruction, which will make it possible for the world to recover in a sustainable fashion.

---

[64] Schumpeter, J.: 'Business cycles', McGraw-Hill, New York (1939).

For the older countries, such as in Euroland, it is imperative that they adjust. They should take advantage of their potential by making better use of their innovation capabilities, by getting rid of their rigidities, and by quickly adopting the new rules of the game. Following in the footsteps of the United States, let them also consider the Asian crisis as an opportunity, in particular, in terms of direct investment.

9
De-Leveraging and the Ideal of Popular Capitalism

'*Neither a borrower nor a lender be*' (Polonius to his son, Laertes)

Over-indebtedness is both an enemy for sustainable growth and the stuff of which bubbles are made, not dreams as found in Shakespeare, but real estate and stock market bubbles.

Over-indebtedness was instrumental in causing the Crash of 1929 and then the Tokyo crash 60 years later. It is a malign agent that leaves ruin and misery in its wake, through the well-known link of asset deflation, banking bankruptcies and money supply contraction, which, put together, choke business activity. In a deflationary environment, debts quickly become unbearable, and all economic agents view de-leveraging as an absolute priority. Together with de-leveraging, the urge for restrictive budgetary policies is high on the agenda in such a framework. On the other hand – and it is the positive counterpart of this bitter medicine – central banks have a double duty in this context: initially, to counter deflationary forces by implementing easy monetary policies, and then to bail out the banking system, through appropriate yield curve steepening[65] policies. By labelling these 'accommodating' policies, we mean three things: lower leading rates, a rising money supply, and finally, a depreciated currency. These types of policy are usually positive for equity markets, and for financial markets generally, which makes it possible

---

[65] By depressing short-term rates to ever-lower levels, all else being equal, the central bank increases the differential between short and long rates, and thus helps to steepen the yield curve in order to increase intermediation margins.

to set the basis for an upturn of the real economy, with the usual time lags between markets and the real world.

Necessary de-leveraging

Creditor–debtor secular antagonism

During inflationary periods, debtors benefit from an ever-decreasing value for their debt through monetary erosion, whereas asset prices continue to appreciate. In deflationary periods, the reverse applies: asset prices are falling, whereas debt values do not stop increasing in real terms. This creates a paradise for creditors and rentiers alike. Let us remember here the 'blessed' time when money market funds in France allowed their holders to 'grow rich while sleeping' between 1990 and 1995. No wonder this type of situation led two years later to such slogans as: 'Bounce back: become a civil servant!' If deflation is a rentiers' paradise, a heavy price must be paid by the real economy, in terms of bankruptcies, lay-offs and deterioration of public deficits. This gives creditors the negative aura of someone who benefits from the misfortunes of others. Conversely, industrialists, tradesmen or craftsmen who make good use of their capital while creating jobs are doing a great deal to rebuild the image of the entrepreneur in the eyes of the public. This distrust of public opinion towards rentiers and even towards the concept of debt itself has deep underlying foundations that the liberal revolution will be able to exploit. From then on, 'debt is the enemy!' became the motto of the 1990s, and a universal one at that, encompassing corporations, private individuals, and, in the final analysis, governments themselves.

Precursory role of corporations

Better informed and better armed than private individuals, corporations open the way to the de-leveraging boom. The 'leverage' craze which in the 1980s had been promoted to the status of a lively symbol of managerial prowess, to the point of feeding an impressive wave of LMBOs, suddenly leaves room for the opposite philosophy: financial orthodoxy revisited. In this regard, bank loans are viewed as a true Sword of Damocles threatening the equilibrium of income statements, curtailing the freedom of management teams, leaving them at their creditors' mercy. As we saw above, the latter's power is enhanced by the fact that in periods of deflation the real value of a loan goes up, quickly making the burden unbearable to the debtor. This leads to the growing practice of large companies to commit themselves to the well-known process of 'stream-lining', implying both massive lay-offs and the sale of non-strategic assets, their aim being not only to refocus the company around its core business, but also and mainly to alleviate a debt burden contracted during the 'roaring 80s'. Let us recall the parallel: roaring 20s, roaring 80s...

Private individuals, in turn . . .

In turn, and as soon as they can, private individuals renegotiate the terms of their bank mortgages. The breathtaking fall of interest rates observed between 1990 and 1999 was a strong incentive to do so. Banks, which are too commonly viewed in the role of villain, cannot easily escape from this refinancing spree, although they were themselves the prime victims of the deflationary wave which chopped away some or all of their equity capital through bad loans provisions. The latter in particular can be traced back to the gigantic real estate commitments subscribed to at market top.

This new sensitivity of private individuals to the burden of their financial liabilities goes side by side with an improvement of their general economic culture, notably in terms of consumer behaviour. In a competing and deflationary environment, the new consumer buys less easily than before and looks around for rebates, discounts and promotional sales, while taking up bargaining as a national sport. Individuals tend to behave all the more cautiously when they feel less secure in their job – at least, when they have one.

In short, the harshness of times not only shapes the economic education of the average citizen, but also brings about a questioning of their prejudices, the first of which being the idea that governments have deep pockets, there to be tapped indefinitely.[66] However, not only have

---

[66] The states themselves, after successfully playing their initial stabilizing part, very quickly found the limits of their prodigality.

private individuals started to alleviate their balance sheets, but rentiers also seem destined for a brilliant future. In an article[67] from *Chroniques économiques* of 15 June 1996, Michel Lutfalla raised the possibility that, for the first time in economic history, rentiers may have a chance not to be spoiled. He quoted two reasons in support of his assumption: the first is demographic, as the ageing of populations enlarges the flood of the old voters, where the greatest proportion of rentiers can be found; the second argument stems from 'the markets' tyranny' as the threat of a rise in the risk premium may deter governments from being too prodigal.

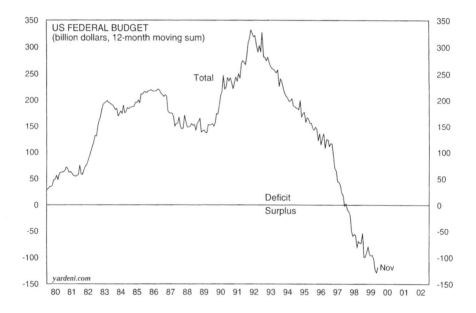

Figure 22. *US Federal Budget. Cumulative 12-month sum, in US$ billion*

Source: Deutsche Morgan Grenfell, 'Weekly economic briefing' of 31 October 1999

---

[67] 'L'impossible euthanasie du rentier'.

Governments themselves on the way to budgetary orthodoxy

The swelling of public deficits, due both to the lengthy down wave that had plagued the world economies and to the subsequent increasing burden of national debts, has triggered sharp reactions of 'regression to the mean' among the main industrialized countries. For fiscal year 1998, the US public balance has turned into a huge surplus of US$76 billion for the first time in decades and following years of steady improvement as shown in Figure 22. In his State of the Union speech on 20 January 1998, President Clinton had initially projected a much smaller surplus of US$10 billion for fiscal year 1998/99. For 1999, the surplus will probably be closer to US$120 billion. Lucky America!

Closer to us, the convergence efforts of the European states within the framework of the Maastricht Treaty have reflected the same concern for breaking away from the devastating effects of over-indebtedness and the excesses of the Welfare State.

Indeed, to reduce public deficits, two solutions can be envisioned:

- Increase fiscal pressure without changing spending growth.
- Reduce spending growth while keeping fiscal pressure constant or slightly declining.

At a time of the long cycle (the depression phase of 1990 to 1997), when in most countries the public sector's percentage share of GDP was considered excessive, it was obvious that the first type of solution could not be considered. The second, on the other hand, had many attractions:

- In the aftermath of the fall of the Berlin Wall and of the subsequent end to the Cold War, an unexpected decline in military spending finally became realistic.
- At the same time, the Reagan method, which consisted in cutting supply lines to extravagant bureaucracies, started bearing fruit at home and being emulated elsewhere: in Britain, Canada, Latin America and Asia.

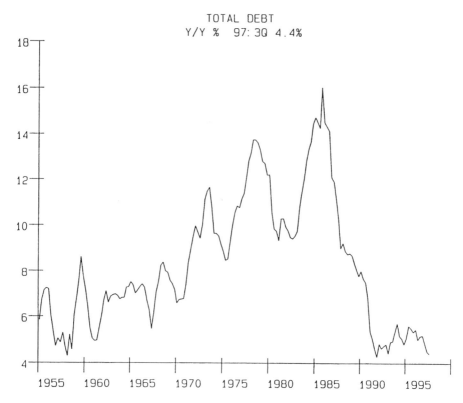

Figure 23. *US total debt (public and private) expressed as year-to-year percentage change*

Source: International Strategy & Investment

De-leveraging calls for monetary reflation

The practice of de-leveraging is deflationary in itself, since it results in a contraction of balance sheets, in particular within the banking system. Combined with restrictive budget policies, it could lead straight to depression if not countered by monetary reflation measures: lower interest rates, rising money supply and depreciation of the currency. Such policies are eminently positive for financial markets, especially for equities.

The return to an equity culture

Whereas debt deflation can be viewed as the catalyst for an economy to slip into depression – especially through rising bankruptcy risk within the banking system – by the same token, the controlled continuation of de-leveraging and the advent of an equity-based economy appears to us to reflect that a country has retaken control of its own destiny. Figure 23, drawn from an ISI publication of October 1997, shows to what extent de-leveraging has been effective in the United States in the 1990s.

We are talking about a fully-fledged revolution. To understand this reversal of mentalities with respect to debt, it is helpful to have experienced the dreadful side of over-leverage, and, especially, of its major consequence, asset deflation. We refer the reader to the description by Irving Fisher of this ominous dynamic in Chapter 3.

In the hardest hit countries, such as Japan and those in Western Europe, private de-leveraging found itself partially compensated by a rise in public debt, at least initially: this phenomenon is clearly established in the case of Japan from 1990 to date. It is less obvious in continental Europe, due to the Maastricht convergence constraints.

All in all, for the governments themselves, and once this role of shock absorber had been fulfilled, the practice during the 1990s was to openly side with the tough stance proponents, with de-gearing and privatizations going hand in hand. For corporations, de-gearing was largely a function of the behaviour of their home stock exchange. In the United States, 'leverage' very quickly left room for new capital issues. In Japan, on the other hand, where very large amounts of convertible bonds with warrants had been issued in the 1980s, conversion was made impossible by the extension of the stock market collapse from Spring 1990 until Spring 1999. Corporate de-gearing was thus made more difficult.

It is with private individuals that the psychological reversal was most radical. With the rise of unemployment and the growing insecurity of employment, the traditional behavioural patterns were upset, to the benefit of saving and investment, and at the expense of consumption and credit. These behavioural changes must be put into perspective with the sociological revolution, which accompanied supply-side policies, the retrenchment of the State, as well as the spirit of free enterprise, and the need to rely foremost on one's own work, far removed from the shelter of welfare. If we add to this the problems of pension funding, then we need to raise the question of popular capitalism.

The ideal of popular capitalism

With the exception of Japan, the practice of restrictive budget policies extended to the entire industrialized world. In Europe, convergence policies were the perfect illustration of that trend, focusing both on a targeted national debt-to-GDP ratio and on capping public deficits. Such policies have had three stimulative counterparts in practice:

- They encouraged accommodating or reflationary monetary policies on behalf of central banks.
- They usually went hand in hand with tax-cutting measures as spending cuts allowed to reduce the fiscal pressure.
- While stimulating the equity market in a privatization context, they enhanced popular capitalism.

The irresistible attraction of equities

From the strict point of view of relative performance, government bonds had been stellar performers in the initial phase of debt deflation, for example from 1990 to 1993 in Japan, when long rates were brought back from 8 per cent to 3.5 per cent, while at the same time in France they fell from 9 per cent to 5.5 per cent. Generally, the profits made on government bonds were so high in the period 1990 to 1998 that they would appear not to be easily reproducible today. On the other hand, with a term structure of interest rates so favourable and a persistent disinflationary trend for prices, equities look like being the favoured vehicle for popular saving – in addition to pension funds. Moreover, all relative performance studies invariably show the superiority of equities over bonds in the long term.

From a demographic point of view, the ageing of industrialized countries raises the issue of how they are going to fund their retirement liabilities ten to fifteen years from now, at the time when a large number of 'papy-boomers' enter the third age. The need for US-style equity-funded pension schemes seems to arise everywhere as a complement to the current redistribution systems.

From a sociological point of view, the small shareholder status had become 'politically correct' well before the fall of the Berlin Wall and the ensuing move towards accelerated privatization of the communist economies. The fact that over the last few years job creations were due exclusively to small businesses has done a great deal to rebuild the image of the capitalist entrepreneur in the eyes of public opinion. The LMBO wave enabling whole or part of the work force to share in the capital of companies has also fared well. With 100 million shareholders from a population of 250 million, the United States looks like a giant laboratory for popular capitalism. But such a spectacular shift of the demand schedule for equities would not have been possible without a symmetrical shift, of the same magnitude, of the supply schedule.

The latter remains potentially infinite. Let us briefly note the needs of emerging markets and countries, the vogue of privatizations within the mature markets and the explosion of venture capital[68] in the growth industries: technology, biomedical, online services, etc.

Popular capitalism, as a new basis for social peace

According to the Chinese leaders themselves, at the time of their XVth Party Congress in September 1997, the distribution of equities to the workers was viewed as a step towards the old communist dream of collective appropriation of the means of production. Who would be more royalist today than the king? Who can ignore today that popular capitalism is a precondition to a new social peace, to a new social contract?

Take the example of France Telecom, where the tranche reserved for personnel at the time of privatization was a great success, in a widely unionized context.

That is why, outside the United States and Britain, it seems important to us to favour equity investments through the development of pension funds, together with the lowering of capital gains taxes, as well as through incentive measures aimed at venture capital and business start-ups.

In this 'new deal' type of framework, two phenomena play a major part: deregulation and privatizations.

---

[68] This has recently benefited from French government incentive measures through specific life insurance contracts with an equity bias.

Deregulation and privatizations at the heart of the creative destruction phenomenon

Until the end of the 1970s, whole sectors of the US economy were still subject to regulation: public services (electricity, gas, telephone), transport (air, ground), oil and gas. Pre-Thatcher Britain was also prone to State monopolies in many areas, such as coal, steel and transportation.

In fact, the deregulation wave can be traced back to 1975, well before the Reagan era, when the 'big-bang' of the US brokerage industry was initiated under President Ford. President Carter, although a democrat and consequently less inclined to reduce the role of the State, presided over the deregulation of airlines (1978), of road transportation (July 1980) and finally of railways (October 1980). President Reagan followed on, first through an Homeric fight against air-traffic controllers, then by dismantling telecommunications giant ATT into several pieces: long distance services and telephone equipment for the new ATT (Ma Bell) and local communication services for the seven 'Baby Bells' (Regional Bell Operating Companies). In addition, he freed domestic oil prices, which until then had been maintained artificially low. In 1984, he carried out the deregulation of natural gas.

In Britain meanwhile, Margaret Thatcher indulged in a privatization craze, her critics accusing her of selling off the 'family silver'. One will long remember the conflict over the coalmines for the social and human scars it left behind.

It is true that all these operations of realignment on international standards have had a destructive effect initially, for they were accompanied by lay-offs and painful reorganizations. In a second step, they have had a positive, creative influence: they allowed the emergence of large internationally competitive groups on the one hand, and of smaller entities, which were taken over by their own employees, on the other. The unused pieces of the formerly protected dinosaurs were put together to create medium to small-sized companies. The latter, once repurchased at low prices by their highly motivated employees and managers, were managed effectively, usually building up networks of new activities, often in the most technologically advanced services or sectors. Their leaders had become their owners, while their employees were now shareholders. The motivation of all was at its maximum and from a desperate plight they had made an enviable company: this was creative destruction at work!

Privatizations had two additional macroeconomic benefits:

- They made it possible for governments to refund their debts by anticipation, very much in line with the spirit of the 1990s.
- They helped the stock market capitalization of their home country grow bigger, and often appreciably – an important strategic advantage in the current universe.

This final comment leads us to move on to our next topic: finance as a source of power and employment.

Modern finance, as a source of power and employment

Naturally, the leading edge that the Anglo-American countries gained in this liberal-prone financial revolution ensured them some superiority initially, especially in terms of relative stock market capitalization. But this superiority was also due to a deeper and broader financial culture at all levels: academic, technical and institutional.

At an academic level, the Chicago School of Finance, a natural extension of neoclassical economics,[69] has spread its paradigms through-out the United States first, then the rest of the world, ever since Markovitz presented his mean-variance optimization approach to portfolio theory in 1952. Other groundbreaking models followed in his wake, including Sharpe's CAPM in 1963, Modigliani-Miller's propositions on capital structure in 1958, and Fama's research on 'efficient markets' from 1965 onwards. Black and Scholes produced their option pricing formula in 1972, in a now world-famous article, which was going to revolutionize the way markets worked for the following three decades. Except for Sharpe and Modigliani, all these names are related to the University of

---

[69] The founding article of modern portfolio theory was Harry Markovitz's PhD thesis in economics presented at the University of Chicago Department of Economics, not the Business School. Milton Friedman is said to have been reluctant to accept the theme, which in retrospect was visionary, as financial research would later blossom in business schools, not economics departments.

Chicago Graduate School of Business, as Merton Miller recalled in a recent article.[70] In a sense, the theory of finance has become more strategic than economic science itself, at least if one compares the amount of research devoted to one or the other over the last 25 years. If anything, one should take a glance at the number of portfolio theory specialists who were promoted to Nobel Prize status in economics over the last few years. After Markowitz, Sharpe and Miller were singled out in 1990, the recent nominations of Robert Merton, Myron Scholes and the late Fisher Black in 1997 have given its letters of nobility to the economics of options and derivative products.

At a technical level, all this research found a powerful echo among Anglo-American investment banks and brokerage houses, whose representative networks cover the planet, and are fed by information agencies, such as Reuters, or by rating companies such as Moody's. The power of these rating agencies can be terrifying, as they can influence the refinancing rates of monitored institutions. This power has been extremely evident at the time of the Asian crisis and again during the Russian debacle.

At an institutional level, in the United States and in Britain, the reality and firepower of capitalized pension funds invested primarily in equities have reflected the outstanding success of a positive, although rationalized, attitude towards risk, which is in sharp contrast with what is going on elsewhere. Their gigantic needs, initially of an actuarial nature, then in terms of asset-liability management, and, finally, of portfolio management and asset allocation, have generated a flourishing and integrated financial services industry.

As can be seen, for many countries much remains to be done in this field, which will remain promising for a long time, because of the ageing of populations in the richer countries.

Finance as the key to future prosperity

With de-leveraging in progress on a planetary scale, and the setting of many meters back to zero, the logic of equity finance is replacing the

---

[70] Miller, M. 'History of Finance, an Eyewitness Account', Journal of Portfolio Management (Summer 1999).

logic of indebtedness, which is much healthier for the real economy. This transformation, which calls for the advent of popular capitalism – itself a precondition of social peace – is promoting modern finance to the envied status of admiralship of economic decision-making, at the kernel of the job creation machine.

Titanic mergers of the Worldcom/MCI kind, or SBC/UBS in the Autumn of 1997, helped make it clear to socialist governments around the world that their domestic industrial champions, being under-capitalized, might be ideal take-over targets for foreign giants. It sometimes helped them change their mind in terms of promoting domestic pension fund industries. By the same token, popular capitalism has often become the order of the day.

10
Signs that the Down Wave is Over

Other women cloy the appetites they feed, but she makes hungry where most she satisfies (Anthony and Cleopatra, Act III, 3)

It is easier to analyse the past than to project the future. The intuitive model that we presented in Chapter 2 on the long-term relationships between production, prices and debt does appear, however, to be empirically validated in an optimistic way by the economic and stock market history of the last 25 years, and thus its predictive potential should not be underestimated.

In essence, what does this model suggest? Primarily, two things:

- First, with the two evils structurally hampering growth – namely inflation and over-indebtedness – now being largely out of the way, the path is clear for a return to more prosperous days.
- Second, the current phase of creative destruction, which can be viewed as the climax of the down wave that began in 1973, is the prelude to the next up wave of the long cycle, which could last 30 years. In short, the return of the up wave is already at hand.

We have shown how much de-leveraging was in progress everywhere in the world (and particularly in the United States). In terms of inflation, we know that it has been constantly slowing down since 1980. Instead, its opposite, deflation, is still feared today. These two *impedimenta* – inflation and over-leverage – being from now on largely out of the way, nothing 'in theory' now precludes a structural recovery in the growth cycle. However, the reader won't be satisfied with theoretical arguments, and we agree. What we need are tangible, concrete signs that the down wave is over.

We can identify three such signs, respectively in the economic, technological and geopolitical fields.

- On the economic front, the US success story appears to us to be a harbinger of similar developments to come for Europe, Japan and elsewhere. Our arguments focus upon three prerequisites: a consolidation of the banking system, a strong stock market and, finally, the 'golden age' syndrome.
- In the technological field, the advent of the information age is perhaps for us the surest and most visible sign that a new frontier is opening up for growth prospects.
- In the geopolitical arena, the foreseeable efforts of demographic giants such as China and India to catch up with and meet Western living standards are the best guarantee to us of an accelerated boom in world trade for the next 20 or 30 years.

Let us review each of these topics in turn.

Concrete economic signs

Which purely economic signs can be used to recognize that a country has emerged from the down wave? It is our view that there are three crucial portents:

1) The health of the banking system. Until the Asian crisis, the British and US banking systems were flourishing, while Japan's was still ailing, and Europe's in convalescence. Being the first victim of debt deflation, the banking system is also the prime beneficiary of the yield curve steepening policies normally decided at the onset of the depression phase by monetary authorities. Remember, the purpose of it all is to lower short rates decisively below the long rate level in order to restore to the system its traditional and profitable intermediation role. By doing so, the central bank allows the banking system to perform profitable carry-trade operations between short-

term instruments and government bonds. By quickly recognizing that this was the way to fix the S&L problem in the early 1990s, Alan Greenspan can be singled out as the smartest central banker of the whole period, while the most timely in his 'accommodating' stance. Because the banking system is the necessary footbridge between the financial world and the real economy, it was of the highest strategic interest, at the beginning of the 1990s, to recognize this vital link as early as possible and consequently to give absolute priority to bank bail-out schemes. Unfortunately, Japan still suffers today for failing to recognize that link early enough, even if its monetary policy U-turn of mid-1995 showed that Greenspan's lessons had eventually been understood. Indeed, on the eve of the summer 1997 Asian crisis, Japanese banking stock prices were on the rise, giving a clear signal that the crisis might be over. The Japanese VAT hike of 1 April 1997, as much as the ensuing Asian crisis, could not have happened at a worse time.

Whereas US and European banks were not heavily committed in Asia, Japan was the most exposed, with total assets of US$250 billion in the region. Out of those, however, the vast majority related to loans to large domestic companies operating overseas. Internal bad loans, on the other hand, amounted to US$500 billion, a figure more recently raised to US$800 billion.

If accumulated losses of the banking system over the last eight years have been abyssal, they may have been partially compensated for by exceptional profits resulting from yen carry-trade operations starting from the summer of 1995. At that time, the Bank of Japan reduced its short rates to 0.5 per cent and let the yen fall against the dollar. Over the following three years, yen carry-trade operations proved very fruitful. The idea there was to borrow in yen at close to zero and invest in dollar instruments at 6.5 per cent initially and around 5 per cent later. Over the next three years, the exchange gain amounted to close to 70 per cent, not to mention the underlying capital gains due to declining long rates. Needless to say, most US arbitrage funds have benefited from this bonanza. However, it does not seem irrelevant to assume that a few Japanese institutions may also have taken part in the ride, given that Japan is a huge net creditor versus the rest of the world, somewhere between US$900 billion and US$1000 billion, and thus a major dollar asset manager.

Without suggesting that the figures above could compensate in any way for the banking losses – which would be absurd – they do, however, underline that Japan's problems are commensurate with Japan's underlying wealth, and thus manageable. We are happy to add that ever since Keizo Obuchi's appointment as Prime Minister in July 1998, the MOF-prepared bank bail-out scheme has become the government's absolute priority, including bad debt write-offs and capital infusions from the government. This programme was greeted positively by the international investment community.

2) The rise of the stock market, which, one should note, is closely related to the first, with the financials traditionally playing a leading role vis-à-vis the rest of the market. Consequently, the rise of banking and brokerage stocks is a harbinger of a general rise in the index, the latter itself heralding an economic revival. In this respect, the performance ranking of the major stock markets since the Gulf War is informative as to which geographic area performed best: once again, Japan is the laggard and the United States is the clear winner (see Figure 24).

So in the winter of 1998/99, the burden of proof was once again left with Japan through the Tokyo Stock Exchange's expected performance. Should it take off now, we thought then, it would anticipate both the happy outcome of the Ministry of Finance's bank bail-out scheme and subsequent economic recovery. What were the chances of such an outcome in the immediate future? In early 1999, most technical indicators favoured a rebound in the stock market, especially with the absence of competition from fixed income securities with ten-year bond rates reaching 0.8 per cent in early December 1998 – an all-time record! In the same vein, we could stress an exceptionally attractive risk premium by historical standards, an accommodating monetary policy, a cash mountain and widespread negative sentiment among investors, which were very good signs. Paradoxically, the signal of the take-off would probably be given by a steep rise in long rates, for it would indicate the beginning of a portfolio shift towards equities. Curiously enough, at the

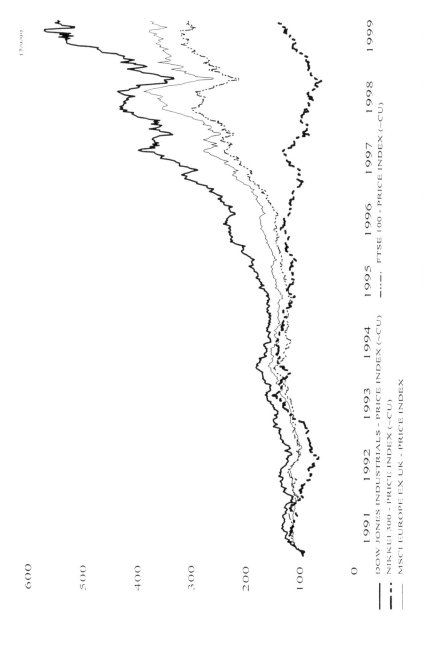

Figure 24. *The compared performances of Dow Jones, FTSE, Index MSCI Europe ex UK and Nikkei*

Source: DATASTREAM

end of 1998 there was a spike in the 10-year bond rate from below 1 per cent up to 2.4 per cent. Needless to say, we greeted this move positively when it occurred. At the end of 1999, the Tokyo market had risen by more than 46 per cent, with a 30 per cent rise in the yen against the euro – the best performance of all major markets.

3)   The 'golden age' syndrome as witnessed in the United States. What do we mean by this provocative formula? It is about the rather rare combination ('once or twice per century' according to Greenspan in his semi-annual testimony to the US Congress of 22 July 1997) of accelerated growth and a concomitant deceleration in prices. Usually, the extension over time of an expansion phase of the business cycle coincides, as is underlined in Appendix I, with rising inflation-ary pressures, but not in this case, as we observe in the current US situation an almost perfect symmetry with the 1970s. At the time, shortly after the first oil crisis, as growth decelerated, a dynamics of scarcity supported an acceleration of inflation. We were losing then on both counts, during that 'rust age'. Today, we see the reverse: the US boom, largely based on technological change and the Microsoft revolution, is a deflationary boom: a 'golden age'. Even if this golden age were to be transitional, what we feel is that another era is coming, from which the United States has certainly felt the early benefits, but whose vocation is universal. It would, of course, be a great satisfaction in the future to see our empirical model validated, as it breaks up the world Kondratieff cycle into three successive waves with a seven- to ten-year lag:

a)   The growth or production cycle, with its apogee in 1973, and its low point in 1997 (we think).

b)   The price cycle, with its peak in 1980, and its trough still to come: 2002 to 2005?

c)   The debt cycle, with its tide of the century in 1990, and its ebb still way out in front of us: perhaps 2015?

However, if the United States gives us today the same signs of a golden age that Greenspan had welcomed just before the Asian crisis broke out, there is no doubt that the same pattern would apply tomorrow to Germany and France, and the day after tomorrow to Japan. In any case, the US example suggests that the current recovery, if it is confirmed, will not be an ordinary recovery, but more the beginnings of a major ascending cycle. This cycle will be carried by two powerful engines: the first is technological change, the second is geopolitical revolution.

A technological revolution comparable in scope with the invention of the printing press

Kondratieff himself had underlined it in his founding article of 1925: each new up wave of long duration is identified with technological change of great magnitude, ie. the steam engine, the railways, electricity, the automobile, etc.

We do not claim to account for the current technological change comprehensively and extensively but we intuitively feel that, in importance for the future of mankind, it matches the Great Discoveries (1492) or the invention of the printing press. It might even be 'oversized', probably for an ordinary Kondratieff cycle, and would rather be appropriate for a much longer super-cycle, of the 500-year type.

Thus *a fortiori* it seems to qualify as an inescapable sign that the down wave that started with the oil shock of 1973 is almost over.

A technical exploit

The technical breakthrough of the years 1980 to 1995 can be summarized by the combination of three ingredients: progress of the personal computer in itself (hardware), the expansion of the user-friendly software industry (software) and the combination of computers, telecommunications and video leading to the multimedia concept.

Let us discuss the first. Since the creation of the personal computer in the 1970s, the technology of the kernel of these machines, ie. microprocessors, has not ceased improving at exponential rates. These chips are the data processing and computing brain of the system, as opposed to peripheral devices intended for storage. The evolution over time of the performance of these chips, in terms of computing speed, which is measured in MIPS (millions of instructions per second), is shown in Figure 25.

Computer Price Deflation

Year of Introduction	Device	MIPS*	Price $	Price Per MIP $
1975	IBM Mainframe	10	10,000,000	1,000,000
1976	Cray 1	160	20,000,000	125,000
1979	DEC VAX	1	200,000	200,000
1981	IBM PC	0.25	3,000	12,000
1984	Sun 2	1	10,000	10,000
1994	Intel Pentium	66	3,000	45
1995	Intel Pentium Pro	300	6,000	20

* Millions of instructions per second

Figure 25. *Evolution of the power and price of microprocessors*

Source: PC Graphics & Video

The cultural challenge of this technical breakthrough

This technical breakthrough opens a double cultural challenge, which is still far from being won, but which should stimulate the enthusiasm of younger generations:

• The true democratization of knowledge and culture.
• The democratization of creativity.

On knowledge, the access to information being almost free, what we have here is a Gutenberg-type revolution, but far more radical still. We now have all of mankind's knowledge at our fingertips and we do not see what could stop the progress of the Internet wherever in the world, whatever the religious, social or ideological barriers.

Illiteracy elimination programmes within the least advanced countries, on the one hand, and the education reform projects of the most advanced, on the other, will both have to be re-examined. More than ever, the education and training of youth and the 'recycling' of adults become absolute budgetary priorities.

On creativity, let us stress that the extension of knowledge, culture and the wider use of sophisticated tools naturally stimulate creativity.

The addition of intellectual content to most or all tasks will raise their status and increase their added value. Moreover, wherever knowledge and technical know-how are on the rise, productivity increases, extending further the limits of scarcity.

Big money at stake

The new frontiers to be discovered are virtual borders; new spices and noble metals are mines of unexploited data. The phrase 'data mining' is not a vain one.

The latest technological breakthroughs open avenues to economic expansion. What is at stake is the rush for the still virgin space of tertiary activities in a world where, thanks to the Internet, the planetary agora has remained on a human scale. Let us rapidly quote here some of these avenues: cyber-commerce, education, training and leisure. So many books having already been devoted to these themes, there is no need to elaborate on them here. Suffice to say that the potential of the multimedia revolution seems to serve our demonstration well.

Lastly, as a major mover of the next up wave, we now have to tackle the question of the extension of development to a new group of countries: the widening of the Kondratieff club tends to proceed by discontinuous leaps with each new ascending wave of the cycle. It is a truly recurring geopolitical revolution.

Geopolitical revolution: the extension of development to a new set of countries is not called into question by the Asian crisis

In an article in the *Revue d'Economie Politique* of December 1979, entitled 'Birth of an economic zone in Asia', we wrote that if the standard of living in Hong Kong had spread overnight to continental China, the latter would have had, at the time, a GDP equivalent to that of the United States – the same exercise, in December 1999, would undoubtedly lead to an estimate of double or triple the GDP of the United States.

This brief example illustrates how quickly the catch-up phenomenon is unfolding between the richer countries and their emerging challengers, in Asia as well as in Latin America or Africa, not forgetting the 'transition' economies from Eastern Europe.

Moreover, until summer 1997 Asia in particular was presented as the engine of the world, the most promising zone in terms of growth and the blueprint of where it was vital to be. It was for our model an outstanding argument, largely supported by the quarterly publications of the World Bank and the International Monetary Fund (IMF). Do the stock exchange, real estate and banking crises, which began in Southeast Asia and South Korea in summer 1997 as a delayed echo of the Japanese crash of 1990, call into question both these prospects and this wonderful argument?

We do not believe so for three reasons. First, because the dynamics of the emerging world, on the eve of the Asian crisis, could be viewed as an independent 'long up wave', with a lead time against the G7 major cycle, itself in the last stage of its depression wave. Second, because the causes of this regional crisis, although major, are but the delayed echo of the Japanese crisis, of which Tokyo holds the key. Finally, because there is an 'objective complicity' between the richer countries and the new countries to manage this crisis with a view to achieving prosperity for a long time.

The dynamics of the emerging world on the eve of the Asian crisis

The statistics speak for themselves. The Third World, and singularly Asia, had for several years entered the up wave of a long cycle. According to the IMF, for the sole emerging countries of Asia, real growth approached 9 per cent per year from 1990 to 1995. Growth totalled 8 per cent in 1996 and fell to 6 per cent in 1997, despite a quasi stagnation in Thailand. In South Korea, Malaysia and Thailand the slowdown had been significant since 1996.

In addition, as stated in the Prologue, the latest forecasts of the World Bank for the year 2020 remain very optimistic, with an anticipated doubling of developing countries' weight in world output, moving from a sixth to a third.

The delayed echo of the Japanese crisis

Thus, logically, the summer 1997 crisis did not have the characteristics of an end-of-cycle crisis, Japan-style, of which it was the delayed echo. We would rather label it a blip of creative destruction, linked to the Japanese problem.

It should first be stressed that, at the end of 1997 at least, the Asian crisis was geographically limited to five countries: South Korea, Indonesia, Malaysia, the Philippines and Thailand. The area's heavyweights, such as China, India, Taiwan, Hong Kong and Singapore, had by and large been kept away from the cyclone, even if they effectively could feel the prevailing wind.

Its causes were primarily of a business-cycle nature: industrial and real estate over-investment, falling competitiveness, swelling current deficits, external financing problems, and, finally, abandonment of the dollar peg.

This last factor alone, by triggering imbalances between deflating assets and inflating liabilities, made the summer 1997 crisis a delayed echo, and a weakened one at that, of the Japanese crisis. That is why Japan undoubtedly holds the key to its outcome, as we saw earlier, and will probably take advantage of that regional challenge to address its own problems head on; those problems have been around for the last eight years, but we saw earlier that Obuchi's government has taken the right steps to bail out the banking system, a move the Nikkei index has started to welcome.

Economic complicity between rich and emerging countries

The bad news has been widely advertised and discounted. The good news has not. 'Good news number one' is that the two heavyweights of the world economy, namely North America and Europe, have grown at an annualized clip of respectively 3.9 per cent and 3 per cent, with no inflation in 1998. In 1999, their growth rates will probably be close to 4 per cent for the United States and above 2 per cent for Europe. Together, these two entities represent two-thirds of world GDP. The 'good news number two' is that Japan has shown significant progress toward addressing its problems. The third is this objective complementariness between rich and newly industrialized countries. Beyond the short-term cyclical side of it, already noted in the Prologue, with Asia's strong export-gearing benefiting from their currency devaluation and from the United States' and Europe's good growth presently, we want to stress the longer-term potential of this solidarity: the wealthy ones, with an ageing demography, are potential providers of capital, technology and know-how, whereas the others, although lacking capital, can rely on a young, hardworking demography with a great desire to fill the gap with the West.

Conclusion
Breaking the Waves with Alan Greenspan: Tomorrow, the Next Up Wave

For a long time, stock market economists and investors have sought to explain industrial and financial phenomena by a sequence of cycles whose periodicity can go from one year (as in seasonally adjusted) to several years, several decades, or even centuries. A better knowledge of cyclical phenomena naturally allows investment professionals to refine their forecasting methods. Given that the future lends itself little to linear extrapolations, the pride of forecasters lies especially in their capacity to anticipate inflections or even reversals. However, if it is very difficult to predict business cycle reversals, it is paradoxically easier to anticipate the long wave fluctuations of our economies! *It is precisely the purpose of this book to foretell the near end of the long down wave started in 1973 and the advent of the subsequent up wave.*

How do we demonstrate it? We use a proprietary model of the relationships between long-term fluctuations of production, prices and debt. We thus describe three long waves – or bell-shaped curves – of around 56 years each, but with a seven- to ten-year lag between them in this order: volumes, prices and debt (please refer again to Figure 1). As production leads and as the down wave naturally begins with the production peak, it is of paramount interest to sketch the 'topography' of a typical down wave in relation to prices and debt. In other words, much of our work lies with the *spectral* analysis of a typical down wave such as the one that hit in 1973 through the oil crisis. We found that a crisis of such a long duration can be broken down into three steps:

147

1) Between the production peak and the peak of prices, the plateau of stagflation.
2) Between the peak in prices and the crest of debt, the 'financial bubble' years.
3) When the needle of debt pierces the bubble, the slide towards the 'creative destruction' step usually associated with depression.

Meanwhile, what we implicitly suggest here is that once the third phase has come to an end, the following up wave is ready to start – hence our invitation to look way ahead of our time, 'beyond the valley'.

In practice, how does this three-step model fit in with reality? The answer is: incredibly well, with the exception of one notorious mismatch. Let us elaborate first on the positive side of the equation before we deal with the 'mismatch' story.

Why then did our model fare so well in light of recent evidence? We showed at length in Part Two (from Chapters 4 to 7) that the test of history is more than convincing, in particular in the detailed parallel between the periods 1913 to 1937 on the one hand and 1973 to 1997 on the other.

In short, twice this century the industrial world has gone through a 'stagflation' phase – first in the 1910s and again in the 1970s – and then through a 'feel-good/bubble year' type era – first in the 1920s and again in the 1980s. And this is true for all major economies. Now, regarding the depression step, most countries have gone through it twice, especially Japan, which is a textbook case. And this makes us feel confident that our model basically holds true and that the deterministic side of the Kondratieff-wave can't be ignored and must be reckoned with.

However, there is a spectacular mismatch or anomaly in our story. For not only did the United States avoid a fall into depression in the 1990s, but it also experienced meanwhile its longest peacetime expansion of the century! Who is to blame for this? Who did the trick? Who tamed the wave? Once again, the answer is Alan Greenspan. Not only did he learn from Irving Fisher that 'depressions are avoidable', but he also had the guts to put the concept into practice – and in case he didn't read Fisher, he must have outguessed him.

Thus we are left with three exciting conclusions:

- First, the world economy is due for another up wave of long duration, of the type last seen in the aftermath of World War II. This is based on the fact that economic history repeats itself and that the inform-ation age will be the prime mover this time. Recent evidence documents 50- to 60-year long Kondratieff cycles, with up waves and down waves of about equal duration, and with inflation and debt excesses viewed, in Fisher's words, as the two evils hampering growth.
- Second, in this respect, the experience of the 1990s has been one of 'creative destruction', a concept usually associated with depression as the last and climactic stage of down waves. Its purpose is to clean up previous inflation and leverage excesses and pave the way for the following technological revolution. In this context, depressions are the usual signal that the next up wave is looming.
- Third, Greenspan emphatically proved in the 1990s that, even if down waves can't be escaped overall, depressions can be avoided. Thus, creative destruction can be made to work in your favour. In other words, the clean-up process can be shortened by adequate monetary policies and depressions need only be endured as worst-case scenarios. Hence, what the world needs in the future will be central bankers able to tame the wave, 'à la Greenspan'.

To sum up, since the early 1990s we have gone through the reality of a depression, which, unevenly distributed as it is, has its epicentre in Japan. We know that it must last approximately seven years and mark its imprint on the whole decade, just as in the 1930s. In common with Janus, depression is double-faced: destructive on one side, creative on the other, which qualifies it as both a painful and privileged transitional period. This duality is typical of the 1990s, which began with a series of major upheavals in most areas, geopolitical, financial, economic, social, cultural and technological. However, these 'seven lean years' have elapsed and what we now expect for the world is 'fat cows time' or the advent of another phase, which has already started in the United States at least and which can be best described as growth without inflation, the 'golden age' of 'new era economics'.

Aside from the United States, which has led the way, the world at large is also cleaning up its leverage excess of previous decades, through a return to basic disciplines, through a fitness treatment and through an increasing role being given to private initiative. In addition, technical progress is opening new virtual borders, even more promising than the discovery of continents with spices galore and abundant natural resources. Information is the new source of wealth and digitized databases are the new gold mines.

The rising aura of the information age thus confirms the conclusions of our mechanistic model, suggesting the nearest end to the current down wave. What remains for us to tackle is the question of its probable timing, which reminds us of the lag we assume in our model between prices and volumes.

Whereas in 1973 the beginning of the crisis coincided with a production slowdown and an acceleration in price inflation, this time, in 1999, the end of the crisis will have to be characterized by the opposite syndrome of growth acceleration and continued disinflation. Once again, this is precisely what we observe in the United States, avant-garde of the world cycle and laboratory of the 21st century.

At a time when Japan doubts itself, when a united Europe is being born through a painful process, and when French society seems discouraged and lethargic after a quarter century of various successive shocks (economic, sociological and political), this book is, once again, a message of hope. Although written from the experience of a stock exchange specialist, it is aimed in fact at all layers of society: students, workmen, craftsmen, industrialists, tradesmen and the unemployed. All must adapt to the requirements and the promises of the post-industrial era, where information will be in the form of both raw material and finished product, work and leisure, constraint and freedom, supply and demand, knowledge and creation. We enter the world of knowledge, whereby, matter being better domesticated, intellectual education will be most sought after, and will indeed become the virtual stake of the rush to prosperity. Naturally, this structural change is not painless, but stands as a remote echo of the rural exodus of the beginning of the century. Paradoxically, this new world order will bring us closer to nature, and not the reverse: the ability to work from one's home will develop and offices will mushroom all over the countryside very much along Alphonse Allais's prescient dreams!

The United States shows us the way and finds followers, both in Asia and Latin America, which are more eager than continental Europe or Japan to take up the challenges of the future. It is true that even in the United States poverty has still not been banned. But one should believe in the driving force of the long cycle that we already see at work there. At the top of the pyramid stand the jobs with highest added value, which by extension generate around them less–qualified employment, including 'small jobs' in a pyramidal way. The long cycle should push the whole pyramid upwards and little by little irrigate even its bottom of gratifying content.

That is why one should not believe that the 'End of Work' has arrived.[71] One should rather believe, conversely, in the increasing democratization of creativity and in the growing ennoblement of all tasks.

The entire planet is moving towards more creative and more prosperous times: will we, particularly in Europe and France, remain on the sidelines?

We do not think so, for we believe that the cosmogony presented here will unabatedly follow its deterministic course, except for some random noise observed locally. This apology for pendulum mechanics has been borrowed from elementary signal theory and is aimed at novice investors. In this empire of waves, which Fourier with all his mathematical apparatus would not have denied, the sine curve is queen. It not only describes the vital pulsation of the four-year business cycle, with its peaks and troughs, with its pauses and contractions, but it also lends its beautiful shape to reflect the secular impulses that agitate the world economy. In our model, all main parameters – production, prices and debt – unfold as dictated by their undulating destiny, while describing perfect sine curves, with time lags though between them, which we justify both by sheer logic and accurate historical record. When we say determinism, what we have in mind is the general trend, which by no means precludes local deviation around the trend – the white noise factor – that leaves room for dreams and freedom.

---

[71] *The End of Work* by J. Rifkin, Putman Publishing, 1995.

It is on this basis that we are looking forward to climbing the next up wave. We suggest labelling it 'Greenspan's Up Wave' for no one else was more instrumental in shaping up *the golden age we find ourselves living in*, as recalled at the onset of this book from Phil Gramm's Senate nomination address.

Epilogue
Alan Greenspan's Brave New World

Miranda: O wonder!
         How many goodly creatures are there here!
         How beauteous mankind is! O brave new world
         That has such people in'it!
Prospero: 'Tis new to thee.

(The Tempest, Act V, scene 1)

Who would be best qualified than our modern Prospero to comment and elaborate on the on going information revolution, which in retrospect will sound as a remote but most relevant answer to all the Mirandas of this world? Let the readers judge by themselves:

'In testimony before this committee several years ago, I raised the possibility that we were entering a period of technological innovation that occurs perhaps once every fifty or one-hundred years. The evidence then was only marginal and inconclusive. Of course, tremendous advances in computing and telecommunications were apparent, but their translations into improved overall economic efficiency and rising national productivity were conjectural at best. While the growth of output per hour had shown some signs of quickening, the normal variations exhibited by such data in the past were quite large. More intriguing was the remarkable surge in capital investment after 1993, especially in high-tech goods, a full two years after a general recovery was under way. This suggested a marked increase in the perceived prospective rates of return on the newer technologies.

That American productivity growth has picked up over the past five years or so has become increasingly evident. Nonfarm business productivity (on a methodologically consistent basis) grew at an average rate of a bit over 1 per cent per year in the 1980s. In recent years, productivity growth has picked up to more than 2 per cent, with the past year averaging about 2.5 per cent.

(Alan Greenspan, 22 July, 1999.)

Four or five years into this expansion, in the middle of the 1990s, it was unclear whether, going forward, this cycle would differ significantly from the many others that have characterized post-World War II America. More recently, however, it has become increasingly difficult to deny that something profoundly different from the typical postwar business cycle has emerged. Not only is the expansion reaching record length, but it is doing so with far stronger-than-expected economic growth. Most remarkably, inflation has remained subdued in the face of labour markets tighter than any we have experienced in a generation. Analysts are struggling to create a credible conceptual framework to fit a pattern of interrelationships that has defied conventional wisdom based on our economy's history of the past half century.

When we look back at the 1990s, from the perspective of say 2010, the nature of the forces currently in train will have presumably become clearer. We may conceivably conclude from that vantage point that, at the turn of the millennium, the American economy was experiencing a once-in-a-century acceleration of innovation, which propelled forward productivity, output, corporate profits, and stock prices at a pace not seen in generations, if ever.

(Alan Greenspan, 13 January, 2000.)

But how long can we expect this remarkable period of innovation to continue? Many, if not most, of you will argue it is still in its early stages. Lou Gerstner (IBM) testified before Congress a few months ago that we are only five years into a thirty-year cycle of technological change. I have no reason to dispute that, although forecasting the evolution of technology is a particularly precarious activity. It nonetheless seems likely that we will continue to experience vast advances in the application of the newer technologies and their associated increases in output per workhour.

But in gauging pressures on cost growth and prices, the critical issue is not how much of the current wave of innovation lies ahead of us, but how rapidly the exploitation of the newer technological synergies proceeds.

If, using Gerstner's figure, the remaining twenty-five years of the thirty-year cycle of technological change is exploited at a much more leisurely pace than the first five years, the rate of productivity growth will fall. To be sure, the level of productivity will continue to rise but at a slower pace.

(Alan Greenspan, Boca Raton, 28 October, 1999.)

Appendix I
Relationship between the business cycle and interest rates

On the one hand, the industrial production cycle, or business cycle, follows a sinusoidal pattern. On the other hand, we suggested in 1981[1] that the interest rate cycle could be represented by another sine curve over the same time frame. We then had to determine whether these two sinusoids were in synch or not, and if not to estimate the time lag between them.

To determine the relative position of these two curves, there needed only be a bridge at one point. We simply made the assumption that the beginning of the recession phase of the industrial cycle corresponded to the peak of interest rates, thus suggesting a lag of a quarter of a period.

Curiously enough, and fortunately, we might add, this quarter period lag between the two sine curves respected economic logic from one end of the cycle to the other, ie:

(a)   The interest rate peak triggers the recession.
(b)   The recession in turn induces a decrease in the cost of money.
(c)   Once the drop in rates has reached a certain threshold, recovery begins.
(d)   Throughout the recovery phase, rates continue to fall.
(e)   It is only in the growth phase that rates begin to rise again.
(f)   Rates continue to rise in the overheating phase and eventually reach a peak.

[1] Review d'Economie Politique, Paris, December 1981.

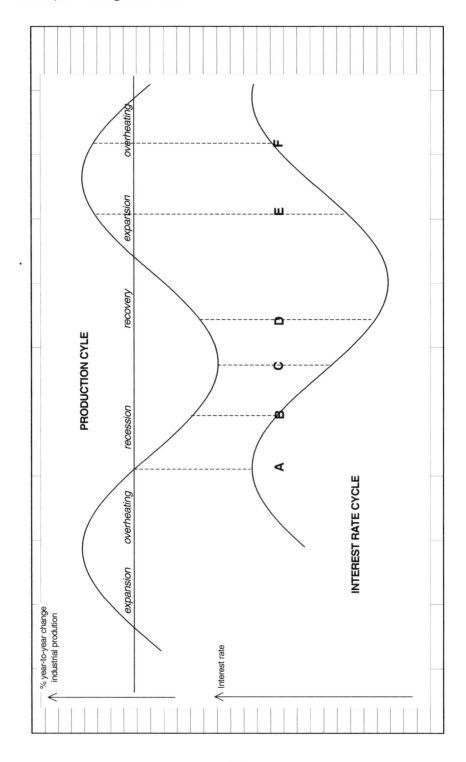

Appendix II
'Are we on the eve of a new stock market crash?'

(Translation of an interview of the author by Liliane Gallifet, *Paris Match*, 2 August, 1990)

Wall Street, July 23rd 1990, there is panic in the air. Within twenty minutes, the Dow Jones Industrial Average, which one week before had gone through the 3000 mark, suddenly loses 109 points. As the Fed comes in to inject liquidity, the slide falls short, to the great relief of investors. The next day, nobody pays attention anymore, except for a few people. Some economists are worried, very worried indeed. On Wall Street, Martin Zweig, editor of the best performing stock market letter over the last ten years, warns that 'within six months the market will be lower'. In Paris, François-Xavier Chevallier, Chief Investment Strategist for BNP Investment Department, is more pessimistic still: 'Rough waters are in store for this coming Autumn. We are on the eve of an unstoppable stock market crash of world proportions, much worse than the previous one. The first area of concern lies with US late cycle threats, as signals of an impending recession have been highlighted there for months. Cunningly, though, Alan Greenspan, Chairman of the Federal Reserve, has managed to postpone it to date. Now, however, the hour of truth seems to draw near, as all indicators seem to converge. Interest rates are going up decisively, at a time when production momentum is losing steam, and housing starts are back to their October 1982 lows; auto sales have been rolling over for the last 18 months, and we already are one year into a profits recession. Indeed since the end of World War II, the US economy has slid into recession several times already, and it has always recovered. In 1987, the underlying business momentum was so quick to erase the economic consequences of the crash that the vigilance of all has been kept asleep ever since'. Why should it be awakened now? According to F–X Chevallier, the answer is 'things are different this time. For this forthcoming interest–led recession is going to collide up front with a debt mountain of unheard proportions in an already deflationary environment. As prices remain subdued, people reckon it is a temporary phenomenon and they will go back up some day. Hence the borrowing binge of the 1980s. As a result, total US debt, including households, corporations and the government, which used to be equal to nominal GDP 15 years ago, has now inflated to twice GDP . . . as much as in the early 1930s. The second area of concern is Japan, where this debt to GDP ratio is threefold, a bit as if on January 1, one had already spent three times one's annual salary. Initially, in the 1970s, debt was raised to buy real assets, such as real estate, gold, paintings, or forestry acreage. Then, in the 1980s, the industrial restructuring wave has fed raiders' appetite for larger and larger leveraged deals. As long as money was kept flowing galore, all went well. But as payment delinquencies have been on the rise, the whole system is seizing up. Ask Donald Trump and Alan Bond about it. Over the last year, problems have surfaced. The banking system has become less eager to finance major deals, and as money is getting scarce, US Savings and Loans are trying to get rid of their real estate assets through auction sales. It looks as if world debt growth has reached a peak. In a context of falling prices and production, the fact that money could become still less available could trigger dreadful chain reactions: a collapse of financial assets, in the first place, then of real assets and its ensuing deflationary and recessionary spiral. Fortunately the worst is not always the most likely outcome . . .'

Paris-Match, August 2, 1990

Bibliography

Aftalion, A: 'Les crises générales et périodiques de surproduction', Marcel Riviere, Paris (1913)

Aftalion, A: 'L'or et sa distribution mondiale', Dalloz, Paris (1932)

D'Arvisenet (Philippe) et Petit (Jean Pierre): 'Echanges et finance internationale, 1. les enjeux; 2.les acteurs', Paris, Banque éditeur (1997); 'Finance internationale, Marchés et techniques', Hachette (1990); 'Les politiques économiques conjoncturelles', Dunod (1999).

Batra, R.: 'The Great Depression of 1990', Simon & Schuster, New York (1987)

Baudin, L: 'Quelques observations relatives à l'influence des variations de la production de l'or sur les mouvements de longue durée des prix', in Revue d'Economie Politique (September/October 1938)

Beckerman, G.: 'Les eurodollars', Paris, P.U.F. (1992)

Beckman, R.: 'The down wave', E.P. Dutton, New York (1983)

de Bernis, G: 'De quelques questions concernant la théorie des crises', Economies et sociétés, Cahiers de l'ISMEA, La crise économique contemporaine, vol xvii, (September/October/November 1983)

Bosserelle, E: 'Quelques éléments de réflexion au sujet des cycles de Kondratieff', Revue française d'économie, vol viii (Autumn 1993)

Burns, A.F.: 'Production trends in the United States since 1870', National Bureau of Economic Research, New York (1934)

Burns, A.F.: 'The business cycle in a changing world', National Bureau of Economic Research, New York (1969)

Chevallier, F.-X.: 'Emergence d'une zone économique en Asie', Revue d'Economie Politique (December 1979)

Chevallier, F.-X.: 'Macro-économie et stratégie de portefeuille', Revue d'Economie Politique (December 1981)

Chevallier, F.-X.: 'Politique de l'offre au Japon', Revue d'Economie Politique (June 1982)

Chevallier, F.-X.: 'Sommes-nous à la veille d'une nouveau krach? Chronique d'une crise annoncée 1990–2000', unpublished manuscript (June 1989)

Dupriez, Leon H.: 'Les méthodes d'étude de la conjoncture économique et les cycles généraux des affaires en Belgique de 1897 à 191', Bulletin de l'Institut des Sciences Economiques, Louvain (December 1929)

Dupriez, Leon H.: 'De l'influence des mouvements de fond des prix sur la vie économique de 1800 à 1935', Annales de la Société Scientifique de Belgique (January/June 1936)

Dupriez, Leon H.: 'Des mouvements économiques généraux', Institut de Recherches Economiques et Sociales de l'Université de Louvain (Louvain 1947)

Dupriez, Leon H.: '1974, a downturn of the long wave?', Banca Nazionale del Lavoro Quarterly Review, no.126 (September 1978)

Escudier, J.L.: 'Le mouvement long de l'économie: terminologie et options théoriques', Revue Economique, vol 40 (September 1989)

Fisher, I.: 'The debt deflation theory of great depressions', Econometrica, vol 1, Paris (1933)

Fontvieille, L.: 'Evolution et croissance de l'Etat Français 1815–1969', Economies et sociétés, Cahiers de l'ISMEA, vol X (September/October/November/December 1976)

Forrester, V.: 'L'horreur économique', Fayard, Paris (1996)

Galbraith, J.K.: 'The Great Crash, 1929', The Riverside Press, Cambridge (1954)

Garnier, O.: 'La "debt-recession" américaine de 1990–91', Revue d'Economie Financière, no.20 (Spring 1992)

Gide, C. and Rist, C.: 'Histoire des doctrines économiques', seventh edition, revised and enlarged (Paris, Sirey, 1947)

Guitton, H.: 'Les fluctuations économiques' (Paris, Sirey, 1970)

Hanappe, P.: 'Les crises contemporaines: vivons-nous un retournement du Kondratieff ?', Metra (December 1975)

Hertzog R. et al: 'La dette publique en France', Economica, Paris (1990), including Llau, P. and Herschtel, M.L.: 'Dette publique et économie', Chapter 19, pp 413–438

Hyman, E.: 'Weekly Economic Comments', Cyrus J. Lawrence (1975–1989)

Hyman, E.: 'Weekly Economic Comments', ISI (1989–)

Imbert, G.: 'Des mouvements de longue durée Kondratieff', La Pensée Universitaire, Aix-en-Provence (1959)

INSEE (French Statistics Institute): 'Annuaire statistique rétrospectif de la France' (1966)

Kindleberger, C.P.: 'The world in depression 1929–39', The Penguin Press, London (1973)

Kitchin, J.: 'Cycles and trends in economic factors', Review of Economic Statistics (1923)

Kondratieff, N.D.: 'The long waves of economic life', Review of Economic Statistics (November 1935), an English summary of original article published in 1925 in Soviet economic review: Voprosy Conjunktury, volume 1.

Kondratieff, N.D.: 'Les grands cycles de la conjoncture', Economica, Paris (1992). This major work includes the following articles: 'Sur les concepts de statique, de dynamique et de conjoncture en économie' (1924)

'Les grands cycles de la conjoncture' (1928)

'La dynamique des prix des produits industriels et agricoles' (1928)

'Questions controversées d'économie mondiale et de crise' (1923)

Preface by L. Fontvieille: 'Kondratieff et son oeuvre scientifique et Les débats théoriques à propos des mouvements longs'

Kuznets, S.: 'Secular movements in production and prices. Their nature and bearing upon cyclical fluctuations', Houghton Mifflin, Boston (1930)

Kuznets, S.: 'Schumpeter's business cycles', American Economic Review (June 1940)

Labrousse, E.C.: 'La crise de l'économie française à la fin de l'Ancien Régime et au début de la Révolution', Paris, P.U.F. (1944)

Laffer, A. and Seymour, J.P.: 'The Economics of the Tax Revolt: A Reader', Harcourt Brace Jovanovich, San Diego (1976)

Laffer, A., Canto, V.A. and Joines, D.H.: 'Foundations of Supply-Side Economics', Academic Press Inc, New York (1983)

Lescure, J.: 'Hausses et baisses des prix de longue durée', Paris, Domat-Monchrestien (1933)

Lutfalla, M.: 'Aux origines de la pensée économique' Economica, Paris, 1981

Lutfalla, M.: 'Histoire monétaire de la France' Economica, Paris, 1986

Lutfalla, M.: 'Sommes-nous en 1815?', Revue d'Economie Politique, no.2 (March/April 1983)

Lutfalla, M.: 'Sommes-nous à la veille d'une grande déflation?', SEDEIS (July 1985)

Lutfalla, M.: 'La grande stagnation du XIXième siècle', Economica, Paris (1997)

Maddison, A.: 'Les phases du développement capitaliste', Economica, Paris (1981)

Marion, M.: 'Ce qu'il faut connaître des crises financières de notre histoire', Boivin, Paris (1926)

Marjolin, R.: 'Prix, monnaie et production. Essai sur les mouvements économiques de longue durée', Paris, P.U.F. (1941)

Marseille, J.: 'Eloge du nouveau rentier', Albin Michel, Paris (1989)

Marseille, J.: 'Empire colonial et capitalisme français: histoire d'un divorce', Albin Michel, Paris (1984)

Marseille, J.: '1873–1929–1993: La crise économique est-elle cyclique?', L'Histoire, no.172 (December 1993)

Maspétiol, A.: 'Privatisables sans frontières', La Vie Française (13 November 1993)

Maspétiol, R.: 'L'ordre éternel des champs', Librairie de Médicis, Paris (1946)

Miller, M.: 'History of Finance, an Eyewitness Account', Journal of Portfolio Management (Summer 1999)

Molinier, J.: 'Les calculs d'agrégats en France antérieurement à 1850', Revue d'Economie Politique (November/December 1957)

Neumann, M.: 'The rise and fall of the wealth of nations, long waves in economics and international politics', Edward Elgar, Cheltenham (1997)

Norel, P.: 'Cycles de Kondratieff et crises – Une approche épistémomogique', Economies et sociétés, Cahiers de l'ISMEA, vol xxv (1991)

de la Puente, F. and de Ullivarri, F.: 'La intensidad de la crisis actual a la luz de la teoria de los ciclos economicos', Economies et sociétés, Cahiers de l'ISMEA, La crise économique contemporaine, vol xvii (September/October/November 1983)

Rifkin, J.: 'The End of Work', Putnam Publishing (1995)

Rist, C.: 'Histoire des doctrines relatives au crédit et à la monnaie depuis John LAW jusqu'à nos jours', Paris, Sirey (1951)

Rostow, W.W.: 'Les étapes de la croissance économique', Editions du Seuil (1962) (originally published as 'The Stages of economic growth', 1960).

Rostow, W.W.: 'The world economy', London, Macmillan Press (1978)

Rostow, W.W.: 'L'ultimatum de l'an 2000 – Chances de survie de l'économie mondiale', Economica, Paris (1981) (originally published as 'Getting from here to there', 1978)

Schumpeter, J.: 'Business cycles', McGraw-Hill, New York (1939)

Simiand, F.: 'Les fluctuations économiques à longue période et la crise mondiale', Paris, Alcan (1932)

Simiand, F.: 'Inflation et stabilisation alternées: le développement économique des Etats-Unis des origines coloniales au temps présent', Paris, Domat-Montchrestien (1934)

Thomas, G. and Morgan-Witts, M.: 'The day the bubble burst', Hamish Hamilton, London (1979)

Toutain, J.C.: 'Le produit intérieur brut de la France de 1789 à 1982', Economies et sociétés, Cahiers de l'ISMEA (May 1987)

Tsuru, S.: 'Economic fluctuations in Japan 1868–1893', Review of Economic Statistics, also cited by Imbert, G. in 'Des mouvements de longue durée Kondratieff' (1959)

Trotsky, L.: 'On the curve of the capitalistic evolution', Vestnik Sotzial-isticheskoi Akademii, vol 4 (1923), also cited by Imbert, G. in 'Des mouvements de longue durée Kondratieff' (1959)

Van Duijn, J.J.: 'The long wave in economic life', Allen & Unwin, London (1983)

Wolff, J.: 'Histoire économique de l'Europe', Economica, pp.368–369, Paris

Yardeni, E.: 'Weekly economic briefings', Deutsche Morgan Grenfell (1990–)

Index

age wave, and the price cycle   3,
   17–20, 53, 59, 101
d'Arvisenet, Philippe   76
assets
   accumulation   57, 65
   prices   122, 127
   see also financial assets
AT&T   130

Bank of Japan, monetary policy in
   1990s   90, 93, 137–8
banking system
   and the second Kondratieff
     cycle   37
   current health of   136–8
Batra, Ravi   60, 77
Beckman, Robert   77
Berlin Wall, fall of   100
biotechnology   114, 117
Black, Fisher   132
Bretton Woods agreement (1944)
   51, 52, 54, 117
Bundesbank, monetary policy
   95, 96
business cycle
   definition   xxii
   and recessions   25
   relationship with interest
     rates   157–9

relationship with the long
   cycle   28

California, gold discoveries   37
Carter, Jimmy   130
Chicago School of Finance   131
China, equity distribution   129
Clinton, Bill   125
Comptoir d'Escompte   37
consumer behaviour   123
Continental Blockade (1807–14)
   34, 36, 41
corporations
   streamlining policies   122–3
   de-gearing   127
creative destruction
   1990 onwards   50, 118, 149
   after Second World War   xxv
   and the Asian crisis   xx
   associated with depressions
     148
   Greenspan's views on   xix, 87,
     109–10
   in the Kondratieff cycles
     xxvi, 42, 44
   in the production cycle   16–17,
     31
Crédit Foncier de France   37
Creditanstalt of Vienna   37

creditor–debtor antagonism   122
currencies
    devaluation   53
    hard and soft   52
cycles *see* business cycle;
        Kondratieff cycles; life cycle;
        long cycles; price cycles;
        production cycles

debt deflation
    Fisher's theory of   xxiv, 29, 31,
        103, 127
    Japan   88–93
    as prime mover of depressions
        112–13
debt growth   57
    1970s   65
    Germany   95
    Japan   31, 91
    USA   30, 31, 67
    see also over-indebtedness
deflation
    definition   23
    and the first Kondratieff cycle
        35
    Japan   25, 89
    and the second Kondratieff
        cycle   37
depression   xxvi, xxvii
    1990s   56, 98, 149
    benefits   112–19
    definition   23, 24
    in the first Kondratieff cycle
        36
    Japan   90, 91, 93–4, 104
    and the long cycle   25

in the production cycle   16–17
in the second Kondratieff
    cycle   37
in the third Kondratieff cycle
    38–9
see also soft depression
deregulation   129
    USA   130
developing countries
    debt   31
    economic development   136,
        143–6
    financing of new markets   65
    industrialization   117
    predicted economic growth to
        2020   xxi, 144
disinflation
    1980s   64–7
    in the production cycle   11,
        25, 27
Dow Jones index, fluctuations
    60, 61
down waves   xxii, 14
    end of the current one   xxv,
        xxvi, 135–46, 147, 150
    in the production cycle   14–15,
        16–17
Dupriez, Leon   7

economic growth, impediments
    to   xxvi
economic power, redistribution
    98–9
England
    during the first Kondratieff
        cycle   35–6

during the second Kondratieff
cycle   36, 37
equity culture   126–7, 128–9,
132–3
Erdman, Paul   77
eurodollars   65
Europe
economic innovation   119
economic power   99
economic situation in 1990s
95–6
over–indebtedness   125
rise in GDP in late 1990s
145
European Monetary Union
(EMU)   96

feel-good eras   34, 41, 44
1920–29   25
1980–90   50, 56, 59–73, 78,
148
associated with leverage   31
definition   xxii
during the first Kondratieff
cycle   36
during the second Kondratieff
cycle   37
during the third Kondratieff
cycle   38
identification   26–7
and the production cycle   11
financial assets, accumulation   66
financial bubbles   xxvi, 60, 93,
148
financial markets
1980s   59–60

effects of 1973 oil crisis   57
financial sphere   67–8
First World War
effects of conscription   52
effects on global economy   54
effects on inflation   38
Fisher, Irving   xviii, xix
analysis of 1930s depression   39
debt deflation theory   xxiv,
29, 103, 127, 149
as applied to Japan   88–93
Ford, Gerald   130
Forrester, V.   7
author's appraisal of   43–4
France Telecom   129
free trade, US policy   95, 96
French 'rente'   9–11
French Revolution (1789)   19
Friedman, Milton   131n

Galbraith, J.K.   52
Galifet, Liliane   75n, 159
Germany, effects of reunification
95–6
Gerstner, Lou   154
gold, rise in price (1971–80)   57
gold standard   52, 54
golden age eras   43
1990s   xvii
associated with technological
revolutions   15
USA   140–1, 149
Goldstein, Joshua   24
government bonds   128
Great Depressions
1873–96   33

1930s   17, 39
Greenspan, Alan
  achievements   xxviii, 84, 148,
    152
  and monetary policy   xix, 90
  perception of deflationary
    threat   101, 103
  and the savings and loans
    crisis   xvii, xviii, 137
  views on creative destruction
    87, 109–10, 149
  views on free trade   99
  views on Japanese crash (1990)
    93n
  views on strength of US
    economy   86, 107, 154
  views on technological
    revolutions   115–17, 153–5
Gulf War (1990)   56
  as beneficial to USA   94–5
  as catalyst of Japanese crash
    79, 80, 87–8, 92–3

Harding, Warren   57
Hawkins, Humphrey   xviii
Hong Kong, as a trading post   36
Hyman, Ed   4, 60, 75n, 92
hyperinflation   25, 40

Imbert, Gaston   xxiv, 33
Industrial Revolution, and the
    second Kondratieff cycle
    36
inflation
  1973–80   49, 51
  1980s   63

and the age wave   3, 19
  effects of 1973 oil crisis   56
  effects of First World War   38
  Germany   53
  peaks   24, 25
  see also stagflation
interest rates
  1980s   69
  1994 rise   xxiii
  relationship with business
    cycle   157–9
international competition, 1980s
    55–6
International Monetary Fund
    (IMF)   144
international trade, USA's laissez-
    faire policy   95
Internet   114, 117, 142, 143

Japan
  bank assets in 1980s   66
  banking losses in 1990s   137–8
  competition with USA   55–6
  debt growth   31, 91
  deflation   89
  depression   xix, 25, 90, 91,
    93–4, 104
  emergence as world economic
    power   98–9
  expansionist budgetary policies
    97
  price deflation   33
  stock market capitalization
    (1989)   71, 79, 93
  stock market crash (1990)   39,
    42, 50, 64, 75–86, 88

stock market price/earnings
multiple   72
stock market rise (1999)   140
VAT rise (1997)   137
Juglar's cycle   7

Keynes, J.M.   90n
Kitchin's cycle   7
Kondratieff, Nicholas   xix, xxii,
xxiii
theory of the long price cycle
xxiv, 7–11, 53
and up waves   xxvi, 141
Kondratieff cycles   8, 54, 100n,
140, 149
first cycle (1783–1837)   35–6
second cycle (1837–83)   36–7
third cycle (1883–1937)   38–9
author's belief in fourth cycle
xxv, 43–6
Korean War (1950–53)   54
Kuznet's cycle   7

Laffer, Arthur   63, 84n
Lawrence, Cyrus   67, 75n
liberalism   100–1
life cycle, and the price cycle   3,
17–20, 53, 59, 101
liquidity trap   90
LMBOs   113–14, 122, 129
London stock market crash
(1825)   36, 42
long cycles
chronological analysis   xxiv,
33–9
components   xix, 3, 4

definition   xxii–xxiii
models   xxiv
phases   3, 5, 112
predicting major events in
76–9
relationship with the short
cycle   28
thematic analysis   xxiv, 39–43
see also price cycles; production
cycles
Long Term Capital Market
(LTCM)   xviii
Louvre Accords (1987)   70
Lutfalla, Michel   4, 33, 124

Maastricht Treaty (1992)   96,
125, 127
magnificent parallels   xxv
between third and fourth
Kondratieff cycles   49–50
definition   xxvi
Markovitz, Harry   131, 132
Marseille, Jacques   4
marvellous clock theory   xxiv,
xxv, 3, 4, 31
mergers   133
Merton, Robert   132
microprocessors   141–2
Microsoft   140
Miller, Merton   17, 131, 132
monetary reflation   126
Moutet, Anne Elisabeth   75n

Napoleonic Wars, and the first
Kondratieff cycle   36
national debts   125

naval blockades, and Kondratieff
  cycles   41
Neumann, Manfred   4, 24

Obuchi, Keizo   138
oil crisis (1973)   xxiv, 49, 51, 52,
  54, 56, 57
option pricing formula   131
over-indebtedness
  accommodating policies
    121–35
  as a cause of stock market
    crashes   121
  causes   51
  see also debt growth

perestroika   100, 111n
Plaza Agreement (1985)   70
popular capitalism   128–33
portfolio theory   131, 132
price cycles
  and the age wave   3, 17–20,
    53, 59, 101
  Kondratieff model   xxiv, 7–11
  relationship with production
    cycles   23–4, 25
  see also long cycles
price/earnings multiple, Tokyo
  stock exchange   72
privatization   129
  Great Britain   130
  macroeconomic benefits   131
production cycles
  phases   11–15
    up wave   15–16, 40
    plateau   16, 24, 25
    depression   16–17

relationship with price cycles
  23–4, 25
see also long cycles

rating companies   132
Reagan, Ronald
  deregulation policies   130
  supply-side economics   xviii,
    52, 57, 61, 63
  views on free trade   99
Recruit Cosmos scandal   73
reflation
  definition   34
  monetary   126
Regulation Q   68
Rexene   113–14
Rifkin, J.   151n

savings and loans crisis, Greenspan
  and   xvii, xviii, 137
Schmidt, Helmut   96n
Scholes, Myron   132
Schumpeter, Joseph, theory of
  creative destruction   xix,
    109, 118
Second World War, and creative
  destruction phase   xxv
short-term cycle
  see business cycle
Singapore, as a trading post   36
Société Générale   37
soft depression   98
South Africa, gold discoveries   38
Southeast Asia, economic crisis of
  1997   xx–xxi, 144, 145
speculative prosperity *see* feel-good
  eras

stabilizers
    definition   97
    types   98–101
stagflation   34, 40, 41, 44
    1980s   78
    parallels between 1910s and
        1970s   51–7, 148
    in the production cycle   11
stock market crashes   17, 34, 44
    caused by over-indebtedness
        31, 121
    London (1825)   xxiii, 36, 42
    October 1987   60, 69–71,
        110–11
    Tokyo (1990)   xxiii, 39, 42,
        50, 64, 75–86
    Vienna (1873)   xxiii, 42
    Wall Street (1929)   xxiii, 38,
        39, 42
stock market rises   138
supply-side economics
    Ronald Reagan and   xviii, 52
    1980s   59, 61, 63, 64

Tax Reform Act (1986)   63
Tax Revenue Act (1926)   63
technological revolutions   114,
        136
    1980–95   141–2
    associated with golden age
        eras   15
    cultural challenges of   142–3
    Greenspan's views on   115–17,
        153–5
    USA   95, 109
Thatcher, Margaret   130

Third World *see* developing
        countries
Tokyo stock market crash (1990)
        xxiii, 39, 42, 50, 64, 75–86
Treaty of Versailles (1919)   56

unemployment
    1970s   52
    1980s   63
    effects of 1973 oil crisis   56
    USA in 1990s   96
United Airlines LMBO's
        financing deal   84
up waves   xxiin, xxv, xxvi, 44,
        149
    in the production cycle   14,
        15–16, 40
USA
    avoidance of debt-led
        depression in 1990s   84,
        101, 103
    benefits of Gulf War   94–5
    business cycles   7
    Civil War   xxiii, 8, 37
    competition with Japan   55–6
    current golden age era   140–1
    debt growth   30, 31, 67
    debt load on banks   68–9
    deflationary booms   33
    deregulation   130
    public surpluses   125
    rise in GDP in late 1990s   145
    Tax Reform Act (1986)   63
    Tax Revenue Act (1926)   63
    technological revolution   95,
        109

trade deficits 70
unemployment in 1990s 96
War of Independence (1776–81)
  35
US Federal Reserve
  monetary policy 94
  reaction to 1987 stock market
    crash 111

Van Duijn, J.J. 7
venture capital 129
Vienna stock market crash (1873)
  42
Vietnam War (1965–73) xxv, 53

Wall Street crash (1929) 38, 39,
  42
wars
  associated with devaluation
    53
  associated with peaks of cycles
    xxv
World Bank 144
World Bank for Horizon 2020
  xxi, 144

Yardeni, Ed 4, 90
Yom Kippur War (1973) 41

Zweig, Martin 159